Black Food Geographies

Black Food Geographies

Race, Self-Reliance, and Food Access in Washington, D.C.

Ashanté M. Reese

University of North Carolina Press CHAPEL HILL

This book was published with the assistance of the Z. Smith Reynolds Fund of the University of North Carolina Press.

The University of North Carolina Press has been a member of the Green Press Initiative since 2003.

Library of Congress Cataloging-in-Publication Data
Names: Reese, Ashanté M., author.
Title: Black food geographies : race, self-reliance, and food access in the
    nation's capital / Ashanté M. Reese.
Description: Chapel Hill : University of North Carolina Press, [2019] |
    Includes bibliographical references and index.
Identifiers: LCCN 2018046425 | ISBN 9781469651491 (cloth : alk. paper) |
ISBN 9781469651507 (pbk : alk. paper) | ISBN 9781469651514 (ebook)
Subjects: LCSH: Food security—Social aspects—Washington (D.C.) |
    Deanwood (Washington, D.C.)—Social conditions. | African Americans—
    Washington (D.C.)—Social conditions. | Food supply—Social aspects—
    Washington (D.C.) | Food industry and trade—Social aspects—United States.
Classification: LCC F205.N4 R44 2019 | DDC 363.8/509753—dc23
LC record available at https://lccn.loc.gov/2018046425

Cover illustrations: *Front*: detail of Garin Baker's *28 Blocks* mural (photo by Seshat Yon'shea Walker); detail of *First Harvest* © iStock.com/Tassii; *Washington DC USA Map* silhouette © iStock.com/werbeantrieb. *Back*: Juan Pineda's *Greetings from Deanwood* mural (photo by Seshat Yon'shea Walker).

For my grandmother, Helen Cooper,
my first real-life example of how care sustains us;
for Terrance and Mr. Parker,
who helped shape this book but did not get to see its final form;
and for Nikki,
who taught me to live with curiosity and fervor.
I love each of you. Thank you for going a piece of the way with me.

Contents

Foreword xi

Acknowledgments xv

Introduction 1
Black Food, Black Space, Black Agency

CHAPTER ONE
Come to Think of It, We Were Pretty Self-Sufficient 19
Race, Segregation, and Food Access in Historical Context

CHAPTER TWO
There Ain't Nothing in Deanwood 44
Navigating Nothingness and the UnSafeway

CHAPTER THREE
What Is Our Culture? I Don't Even Know 69
Nostalgia and Memory in Evaluations of Food Access

CHAPTER FOUR
He's Had That Store for Years 91
The Historical and Symbolic Value of Community Market

CHAPTER FIVE
We Will Not Perish; We Will Flourish 111
Community Gardening, Self-Reliance, and Refusal

Conclusion 131
Black Lives and Black Food Futures

Notes 141

Bibliography 149

Index 157

Figures, Maps, and Tables

FIGURES

1. John P. Wymer's hand-drawn map of Deanwood in 1948 23

2. Decline of grocery stores in D.C. 36

3. Grocery stores leave the District for suburban areas 37

4. *Washington Post* article highlights Super Pride's arrival
   in Deanwood 39

5. *Washington Post* follows Super Pride's success, highlighting
   "soul food" as a primary factor 40

6. Fruits and vegetables at Community Market 92

7. Residents and volunteers "wobble" together at the
   Community Planting Day 112

8. A volunteer from SNMA measuring a resident's
   blood pressure 113

9. Plants near the window in Mr. Harris's apartment 117

10. Beginnings of lemon and orange trees in
    Mr. Harris's apartment 117

11. Bricks dumped at the foot of the hill where Mr. Harris
    wanted to plant watermelon and cantaloupe 120

12. Mr. Harris and Reese examining a raised bed 124

MAPS

1. Grocery stores operating in Deanwood, 1925–1960 30

2. Grocery store locations and percentage Black or
   African American population 48

3. Grocery store locations and median income 49

TABLES

1. Changes in the number of confirmed and planned full-service grocery stores in D.C., from 2010 to 2016 50

2. Survey participants' demographics by self-reported income 53

3. Ward 7 residents' open-ended responses about the local Safeway 54

Foreword

What an incredible honor to write the foreword for such a groundbreaking, thoughtful, and important book that I hope will have a far-reaching impact on mainstream narratives around Black communities, food justice, agency, and resilience.

As an advocate, activist, organizer, and overall troublemaker who, for over fifteen years, has worked to build power for Black communities working toward a more just food system, I find it incredibly important to stay abreast of how dominant narratives impact our work on the ground. At best, narratives help frame an understanding of the conditions and systems at play on the ground in real time and subsequently influence how community-based solutions around systemic change are uplifted and resourced. At their worst, dominant narratives perpetuate narrow analyses that often invisibilize community-based assessments of their own conditions and subsequently diminish support for community-based assertions of their own power and solutions.

There are many factors that influence, create, and elevate dominant narratives, but who has the power to interpret, define, articulate, and influence what we understand realities to be lies at the heart of them, including problems and solutions in the food system. We see this in media framing, in those with political power, and within consolidated corporate power that influences both media and politics. We also see the power of narratives coming from the academy and research institutions — the way our communities are studied, assessed, and analyzed with solutions or even narratives surfacing that have broad, far-reaching implications.

No place have I seen this more clearly demonstrated than in how the term "food desert" circulated broadly from a 2006 study sponsored by LaSalle Bank and authored by a prominent researcher based in Chicago. Although the study featured a map that demonstrated the correlation between the lack of grocery store locations and Black communities in Chicago specifically, the mainstream narrative became one of "food deserts" as the problem of "communities who lacked a grocery store" within a radius of a certain number of miles. In this case, not only was race minimized (or erased, actually) in the assessment of the problem, but the subsequent solutions corresponded to the narrow definitions of the problem that resulted from how the study was framed and disseminated. As a result, the community-based solutions I saw and was a part of were often erased or unacknowledged in any of the mainstream policy, funding, or programmatic remedies that followed. Most resources were poured into brick-and-mortar corporations, regardless of their investment in or ownership by Black communities.

In *Black Food Geographies: Race, Self-Reliance, and Food Access in Washington, D.C.*, however, Dr. Ashanté Reese provides us with a long overdue disruption of so many narrow, harmful narratives, particularly around Black communities, and provides a critical opportunity for course correction. Dr. Reese helps us restore the connection between race—particularly Blackness—and the disinvestment of grocery stores (what many of us call grocer redlining) and helps us actually name anti-Blackness as one of the root causes that create the conditions we find in our communities.

Further, Dr. Reese surfaces the notion of "nothingness," which is threaded throughout the book, challenging the broader mainstream narrative to consider the context, history, agency, and actual assets that Black communities embody. We see in this book that these mainstream notions of nothingness— that Black communities are deserted, empty, and lacking—have become internalized by some of our communities, creating harmful regurgitations of narratives perpetuated within and about Black communities. Thank goodness for *Black Food Geographies*, however, because we now have a much more comprehensive narrative and analysis that go beyond nothingness and actually provide a context that is much more helpful, rooted, asset-based, and empowering, that, again, helps to course correct narratives that instigate internal and external limitations of community-based solutions. Dr. Reese's incredibly thorough body of work here affirms what I've observed in my own community work—that Black communities have embodied solutions and created their own foodways for a long time.

Black Food Geographies also helps unpack some of the assumptions, be they overt or unacknowledged, about Black and low-income communities, agency, and good food access. Too many times have I been in local food policy meetings with grocers spouting off some of the most racist, dehumanizing, xenophobic stereotypes around violence, theft, and safety to justify their decision to disinvest in Black communities. These stereotypes and assumptions also extend to other policies, such as the numerous attempts to restrict choices of people who use the Supplemental Nutrition Assistance Program (SNAP), ignoring the structural composition of communities, and solely basing their advocacy around assumptions that low-income communities have no wherewithal to make good decisions on how to spend their resources. Finally, I have witnessed too many organizations, policymakers, and others making many assumptions surrounding low-income and Black communities' understanding of health (or lack thereof), which in turn has driven policy and programmatic remedies built on the erroneous belief that communities have no knowledge, skills, or histories with good food and health. I can't count how many times in the past fifteen years I have heard questions or comments that suggest that Black communities don't want healthy food. Again, Dr. Reese's work here helps to correct and unpack so many of these false assumptions.

All communities are nuanced, and they are never monolithic. As a direct by-product of anti-Blackness, however, mainstream dominant narratives rarely afford Black communities the dignity or humanity of nuance. We are instead often represented in flat, one-dimensional narratives that often have the subtheme of nothingness or lack running throughout. Through the voices lifted up via *Black Food Geographies*, however, we hear directly from communities about how they experience food access in addition to the critical ways in which they create their own foodways and interventions. Because of Dr. Reese's work, we get to hear their voices and their analyses and bear witness to their agency.

What Dr. Reese ultimately does brilliantly in this book is the best of what narratives can offer: helping to frame an understanding of the conditions and systems at play on the ground in real time. May we all pay close attention to, learn from, and study this very important text, and may it have the broad reach that it absolutely deserves. We now have an essential text that we can add to a limited number of food justice texts (actually embodying the justice part), and for that, I am so excited. Here, Dr. Reese helps to brilliantly restore the power and creation of dominant narratives around local foodways to where they should have been in the first place—the people.

Enjoy the brilliance of *Black Food Geographies*. Dr. Reese is teaching us—with great detail, consideration, and so much care—what justice really looks like.

Dara Cooper,
National Black Food and Justice Alliance

Acknowledgments

As I sit to write these acknowledgements in my hometown, I look to my left: the house where my great-uncle lived. To my right: my grandmother's. Down the way: other remnants of those who've gone on to become ancestors and some reminders that there are a few who are left here to go on with the living. My very first lessons in love, in care, in struggle, and in creating ways out of no way were learned here in Cooper Settlement, a small community of mostly family in East Texas. Here, too, were my first lessons in the scars of white supremacy, the legacy of which we grapple with intimately on the land where I was reared. I don't pretend that this place or people here were or are perfect. But the life I live is only possible because of many sacrifices—named and unnamed—that my family (especially my mother, grandmother, and siblings) made so that this curious, hard-headed, empathetic girl could go off and be who she wanted to be. Above all, I give thanks to this land and people, the living and the dead. This book is for you all.

So many people helped this book become a real thing in the world, and I know those I name will only be a partial list. Thank you to my colleagues at Spelman College, especially in the sociology and anthropology department, where I have been consistently and lovingly encouraged in this work. Also, a big thank you to my students, who, at some points, got less of me so that I could give more of myself to the writing process. They inspire me so much, and I hope they are proud. Thank you to those who have extended mentorship to me, especially Rachel Watkins, Sabiyha Prince, Psyche Williams, and Michael Bader, who read multiple drafts, Valerie Johnson, and to Christina Sharpe, whose work and encouragement at the end of this process were a much needed extra push.

I received financial support that was instrumental for completing *Black Food Geographies*. Many thanks to Spelman College for grants allowing me to conduct additional fieldwork and to attend a writing retreat during the initial conceptualizations of this book. The UNCF-Mellon program generously provided a semester leave, during which I was in residency at the James Weldon Johnson Institute (JWJI) at Emory University, where I was supported by a graduate research assistant and was provided space and time to think, write, revise, share ideas, and write some more. Thank you to the JWJI staff—Andra Gillespie, Kali Ahset Amen, Anita Spencer, and Latrice Carter—for creating an environment where rigorous intellectual and care work happened. Deep gratitude and appreciation to the ten colleagues who were also on leave with me at JWJI. Alex, Felipe, Charissa, Ashley, Kyera, Taina, Derek, Justin, Alison, and Amrita, you were great intellectual thought partners and friends. Also, many thanks to the archivists and staff at the D.C. Public Library's Washingtoniana Collection, the Historical Society of Washington, D.C., the Special Collections at George Washington University, and the Food Marking Institute (FMI) for helping me find maps, primary documents, and other data sources that form much of the historical context for the book. Thank you to Emeline who helped create the maps for this book and to Seshat whose photography graces the cover.

There is a fierce group of sister-anthropologists with whom I have laughed, traveled, and/or commiserated with about writing. There are many of them, but I want to especially thank Erica Williams, Bianca Williams, Donna Auston, Savannah Shange, Symone Johnson, Sabiyha Prince, Jamie Thomas, Laurian Bowles, and Hanna Garth for their consistent support and co-labor. Several friends and colleagues read chapters and provided critical feedback: Matthew Thomann, Khalfani Herman, Karida Brown, Walker Swain, Kamela Hayward Rotimi, and Nikki Lane among them. The intellectual work they offered to sharpen my project cannot be overstated, and I feel lucky to be in community with them. In the unexplainable magic of the universe, I met Brandi Thompson Summers just as I began this process. Soon after, we become press mates and writing partners. Thank you Brandi for reading drafts of this work but also sharing in hours of conversations and check-ins that modeled the vulnerability and care I hope to consistently sow into the world. Deep appreciation to Lucas Church, my editor at UNC Press, who—even when I fretted about it being too much of this or too little of that—saw something special when this book was an early manuscript. Thank you to Tamara, who regularly listened to me process my fears over writing and completing this book, and to the teachers and yoga community at Sacred Chill West. To the friends who make up a good part of my daily support system—Dara, KT, Zandria, Jamey, Tauheed, Solana, Natasha, Phillip, Monica, Shana, Jania, and Alba—each of you offered advice and encouragement, listened to complaints, and in many cases offered tangible support when I needed it. A special thank-you to Elizabeth Kennedy—my oldest friend, my most consistent cheerleader, and a person with whom I dream up the worlds we want to live in. I have named some names here, but there are many others. Thank you to the many—near and far—who provided the key thing that sustained me when I was too tired or lacked confidence: love.

And lastly, I have to thank Zora Neale Hurston. You're the reason I am an anthropologist. You're the reason I believe in telling stories, especially those that may not be the most visible. You came to me once in a daydream when I was writing a graduate school paper, encouraging me on this path. I believe you've been with me since.

Black Food Geographies

Introduction

Black Food, Black Space, Black Agency

I sat on Mr. Johnson's front porch on an October afternoon in 2012, an impromptu meeting after another participant in my research, Lawrence, spent two hours walking with me around Deanwood in Washington, D.C., sharing its history and his childhood memories. What was supposed to be a quick introduction turned into us joining Mr. Johnson on his porch, listening to him more than doing much talking ourselves. Lawrence introduced me as a researcher who was studying food access in the neighborhood and asked Mr. Johnson if he had anything he would like to say about that. As it turned out, he had plenty to say. Similar to other elders, some of whom are featured throughout this book, Mr. Johnson had made a life for himself in Deanwood. That life included gardening. There on his porch, he lamented the increasing reach of industrialized food, critiqued what he presumed to be the failures of parents for not teaching their children to eat healthy, and discussed how growing his own food was one way he combatted chronic illness. On his porch, he was the storyteller. We were his audience. Both Lawrence and I, born and reared in the South, deferred to his knowledge and stories out of respect but also out of genuine curiosity. Lawrence had already explained to me how much he admired Mr. Johnson. I wanted to know why.

"You ever eaten green tomatoes?" he asked me in the middle of describing the peppers, tomatoes, and cucumbers he grew in his backyard garden. "I love green tomatoes. I grew up eating them," I replied. He didn't miss a beat. "They have a lot of nitrate in them. You can eat them fried. You ever heard of that—fried green tomatoes?" When I replied in the affirmative, Mr. Johnson continued: "Yeah. Breakfast food. And that's something. Say maybe in the morning, if you don't want to eat meat, you can eat green tomatoes. That'll fill you up, and a bowl of cereal." Our conversation was part agricultural knowledge transmission, part life history, and part life instruction as Mr. Johnson told me about himself while also giving me directives about how to grow and eat good food. His backyard garden was not a public health intervention aimed at Black families and communities to improve health disparities that develop as a by-product of the wear and tear

1

of anti-Blackness on the body. It was not a conspicuously consumed or marketable green space tied to a return to urbanism. Despite how media often tout white-led organizations who "bring good food" while obscuring or ignoring the various ways Black residents have engaged in similar efforts,[1] Mr. Johnson was one of many Black people across space and time (and in Deanwood in particular) who had grown food in cities for generations. It wasn't even an explicitly politically engaged effort. His stories and his garden laid bare practices of everyday life that were neither loud nor attention seeking. He was, like most of his neighbors, simply making a life.

I begin with this conversation on Mr. Johnson's porch because it, along with others during the first four months of fieldwork, altered my approach to the research conducted for this book. Rather, these early conversations changed what I was listening for. It was not because of what Mr. Johnson said but more so *how* he oriented himself toward talking about food and the work I was doing. At the time, my theoretical orientations, heavily influenced by anthropology, food studies, and sociology, were consumed with assumptions about the influence of the built environment on people's lived experiences; that the places in which they lived shaped them or were the backdrops against which life happened. My assumptions reflected a static, unidirectional understanding of the role of place in food access inequities—this despite the fact that I, a Black woman, have lived my life among other Black people who, even in the context of anti-Black racism, do not exist in a unidirectional series of events wherein we have no say over some of the contours of our lives.

During that first meeting, there was no way for Mr. Johnson to know that about my training, but he was, of course, an expert on his own lived experience and what that meant in the context of food. Even though Lawrence introduced me as a researcher who studied food access—"you know, grocery stores and stuff like that"—Mr. Johnson spoke very little about grocery stores during that hour on his porch other than to lament that processed foods are harmful to children. I never found out his own grocery store preferences. Instead, I left with questions about how Black residents connected past, present, and future in their experiences with navigating an anti-Black food system and what tools helped them to do so. The flow of his storytelling—reflecting the cadences, humor, and grandeur often evident in Black oral traditions—revealed what Zora Neale Hurston wrote about in *Dust Tracks on the Road*: that research was the blessing through which I could formalize the curiosities that emerged on Mr. Johnson's porch, and that if I got out of the way, Black people would tell their stories how and when they wanted. It was not my job to dictate which stories should be told, but if I let them, Black storytelling would lead me places that I had not planned to go.

Following the stories and rethinking my theoretical orientations brought me here to this book: one that is deeply engaged with food inequities produced by anti-Black racism but also concerned with how and where Black people create food geographies within and in spite of it. Tensions emerge when the state fails to meet communities' needs and food corporations justify pulling out of or avoiding Black neighborhoods because of high insurance rates, crime, and low sales. While this failure is oftentimes expected by Black people, the contradictions between the "American Dream" that we are encouraged to embrace and the ways anti-Blackness curtails that fictive dream are stark. We have only to look at the uneven development of neighborhoods across the United States, the historic and ongoing disinvestment in cities with Black majorities, and the current global crisis of gentrification to see how these contradictions are embedded geographically, demonstrating that geography is not race neutral. Instead becomes an important analytical component of understanding the limits of the so-called American Dream and the pervasiveness of anti-Blackness.[2]

In the most jarring moments, spectators watch Black death on repeat as video after video reveals unarmed Black people shot down in the streets by officers imbued with power through the state. Though often treated separately, these sensationalized Black deaths are inextricably linked to questions of food access, as these different iterations of structural violence and racial terror stem from shared roots that attempt to curtail Black mobility in and access to public space. Instantaneous deaths at the hands of police like those of Sandra Bland, Tamir Rice, Terence Crutcher, and Keith Lamont Scott are public and incite immediate commentary and sometimes action. In many ways, these deaths are those that insist that anti-Blackness be taken seriously as a frame for understanding the varied assaults on Black life. Others are slow, walking, everyday deaths: the lack of access to healthy, affordable foods, the continuous expansion of multinational food corporations that control not only access but also wages of folks who produce food, and the cutting (and erasure) of social services.

Theorizing racism in the food system deepens our understanding of the extent to which food institutions are implicated in continued disinvestment in Black neighborhoods. Relatedly, studies beginning in the early 2000s have focused on food justice efforts that reveal meaningful, though sometimes fragmented, efforts to combat food injustices. Yet, the everyday lives of people who are neither explicitly calling out racism in the food system nor connected to organizations that attempt to produce change are often rendered silent, running the risk of reifying the very violence scholars and activists seek to eradicate.[3] One of the entry points for this book is that in turning toward the everydayness of anti-Blackness as an analytic for framing the broader structures that produce food inequalities, we theoretically and methodologically challenge assumptions about how food inequities shape Black lives. Though seemingly a small shift, I offer this thinking on anti-Blackness as the condition that produces and reinforces the expendability of Black people have contested across space and time. This opens up possibilities for us to reconsider and imagine constraint and possibility, harm and care, and destruction and community building. If anti-Blackness is, as Christina Sharpe writes, an all-encompassing climate that produces premature Black death and opportunities to tend to those who yet to live,[4] and the precondition for the perpetuation of capitalism as argued by Adam Bledsoe and Willie Wright,[5] then what do we make of those who survive? How do we see, read, and document their food lives within, alongside, and against the food inequities anti-Blackness produces?

In "Black Feminist Futures and the Practice of Fugitivity," Tina Campt explores what she terms "quiet photography," or photographs that capture quotidian practices of the subject or the state. Firmly declaring that "quiet" does not mean the absence of articulation or meaning and that "quotidian" is not synonymous with passivity, she asks, "What practices of rupture, refusal, and futurity do these images show?"[6] In defining refusals within ethnographic research, Carole McGranahan writes, "To refuse can be generative and strategic, a deliberate move toward one thing, belief, practice, or community and away from another. Refusals illuminate limits and possibilities, especially but not only of the state and other institutions. And yet, refusal cannot be cast merely as a response to authority, or an updated version of resistance, or a concept to subsume under already existing scholarly categories."[7] She offers four components for theorizing refusal, cautioning us to read and understand each of them within the specific ethnographic contexts in which we are working: (1) refusal as generative, (2) refusal as social and affiliative, (3) refusal as distinct from resistance, and (4) refusal as hopeful and willful.[8]

Thinking with Campt's notion of quiet and intentional listening to the everyday and McGranahan's articulation of refusal in ethnographic work, *Black Food Geographies* focuses on individual, everyday lives rather than institutional actions and organizing. At the heart of this work are ethnographic stories, some captured in interviews, some captured in informational conversations, and others translated through me as a participant observer making sense of various scenes. For just over four years, I focused on these everyday ways residents navigated food inequities. What emerged are these quiet food refusals: the ways that Black residents expressed agency, care, and dissent in their food procurement practices, in their memories, and in their hopes for the future. These refusals, like those Mr. Johnson expressed, were not loud. They were not hypervisible. But they were valuable. Embedded in the stories included here and others like them are, perhaps, necessary seeds for growing a radically different food system. Thus, *Black Food Geographies* outlines the structural conditions that provide the context for food inequities, but it also examines how residents navigated them. *Black Food Geographies* explores the contours of procuring food by asking, How have Black people been challenged by and resisted unequal food access? How do quiet food refusals show up in everyday life?

Anti-Blackness and the Food System

In 2007, the last remaining grocery chain closed its doors in Detroit, a city that covers over 100 square miles. In the flatlands of Oakland, there is an average of one grocery store for every 93,000 residents.[9] In a 2011 report, the Illinois Advisory Committee to the United States Commission on Civil Rights stated that while low food access occurred in suburbs, predominantly Black neighborhoods in Chicago carried the highest burden, following the residential segregation patterns in housing.[10] Even in a city like New York, one often heralded as a "melting pot," unhealthy food environments are correlated with neighborhoods with higher Black populations.[11] Across the country, Black neighborhoods and cities have less access to grocery retail and fresh, healthy, affordable food than their white counterparts. This book primarily focuses on Deanwood in Washington, D.C., but it could also be about any number of predominantly Black spaces in the United States and beyond.

There is disagreement on how to name and frame this phenomenon. In popular consciousness and policy, lack of access to healthy food has become nearly synonymous with the term "food desert." Food desert was reportedly first used in the UK in the 1990s to describe low-income areas that did not have access to healthy and affordable food. Since then, its use has proliferated, and the term is affixed to spatial contexts across the world. The Economic Research Service (ERS), a department of the United States Department of Agriculture (USDA) developed the Food Access Research Atlas, a mapping tool. In 2011, the ERS defined a food desert as a low-income census tract where a substantial number or share of residents have low access to a supermarket or a large grocery store.[12] Widely used by academics, policymakers, and organizations, the mapping tool created by ERS allows users to apply different distance markers (for example, one-half mile, 1 mile, and so on) and characteristics (for example, vehicle access) to determine if an area is a food desert. The tool itself is useful, giving a broad view of supermarket access in any given city, state, or region. Noticeably absent are demographics such as race that shift the perspective from what a city, state, or region lacks to encouraging users to consider the systemic patterning of food inequities alongside the racial composition of neighborhoods.

"Food desert" captures the imagination. When people hear the term, many imagine a barren, empty place. That is precisely why the term is inadequate when applied to understanding food access. The focus on what is missing in a neighborhood is central to food desert definitions and often manifests in a narrow focus on supermarkets. Further, with the exception of pointing out the overabundance of corner stores, fast-food restaurants, and liquor stores in neighborhoods that have few grocery stores, analyses often exclude other forms of food retail or means for procuring food, resulting in a neatly packaged product with little understanding of processes—macro or micro—that shape access.[13] This has far-reaching implications for Black communities because of social science legacies of writing about them as static, unchanging, and without agency.[14] Lastly, as Samina Raja, Changxing Ma, and Pavan Yadav note, the term itself has been used loosely, perhaps because of the lack of consistent measures and empirical studies.[15]

As activists and scholars critique "food desert" as a descriptive or analytical framework, some employ alternative language that points to systematic processes that intersect with anti-Blackness to disrupt the assumption that the market is neutral, highlighting how race-related food inequities are embedded in processes and policies that negatively affect Black people and communities.[16] Some turn to the term "supermarket redlining" as an alternative to "food desert." In a 2001 article titled "In Poor Health: Supermarket Redlining and Urban Nutrition," Elizabeth Eisenhauer cites articles in *The Progressive Grocer* and *Newsweek* that identify the practice of grocery stores consciously avoiding low-income areas as supermarket redlining. The term "supermarket redlining" predates food desert, but it has much less traction in the academic literature or public use. Naa Oyo Kwate, Ji Meng Loh, and Kellee White draw on similar ideas but explicitly connect the practice of avoiding certain neighborhoods to race, defining retail redlining as "spatial discrimination whereby retailers, particularly chain stores, fail to serve neighborhoods or target them for unfavorable treatment based on the racial composition of the customers and/or the store operators."[17] This is slightly different from how Alison Alkon and Teresa Mares define and frame supermarket redlining. In their work, they draw directly on banks' history of discriminatory lending practices toward Black people.[18]

If supermarket redlining names the actions of supermarkets, then food apartheid names the structural conditions that affirm and normalize such practices. Perhaps unsurprisingly, the term "food apartheid" is much less prevalent in popular language and academic literature, though platforms like the Movement for Black Lives (M4BL) use it in their work toward Black liberation.[19] In an interview with *Guernica Magazine*, Karen Washington offered "food apartheid" as an alternative to "food desert" because it "looks at the whole food system, along with race, geography, faith, and economics. You say 'food apartheid' and you get to the root cause of some of the problems around the food system. It brings in hunger and poverty. It brings us to the more important question: What are some of the social inequities that you see, and what are you doing to erase some of the injustices?"[20] Apartheid brings forth visceral connections to the politically and socially imposed racial hierarchies and inequities in South Africa and forces us to grapple with how the state, policies, and practices normalize inequality.

Though few scholars have applied the term to their analyses, Joshua Sbicca, Katharine Bradley, and Ryan Galt are notable exceptions. Describing "food desert" as a neutral term that maintains the status quo of avoiding talk about systematic racism, Sbicca argues that "'food desert' often leads food activists to lend charitable support to manage the symptoms of the condition, whereas a term such as 'food apartheid' lends itself to an analysis of the structural causes behind the condition."[21] Bradley and Galt argue that food apartheid is more appropriate specifically because of "the racially exclusionary practices that have brought the situation into being."[22] The historical and ongoing significance of race at the intersections of capitalist accumulation, dispossession, and residential segregation requires an understanding of how the geographic distribution of food is a reflection of anti-Blackness and oppression as much as it is about class and economic capital. As explored in depth in chapter 1, the increasingly corporatized food system is not simply unequal; it is a by-product of how structural racism touches every aspect of life—even where our food resources are located.

Black Food Geographies: Self-Reliance and Nostalgia in Everyday Life

Black Food Geographies toggles between macro-level analyses of food apartheid and micro-level analyses of how residents navigate the unequal food landscape. The context described above and elaborated on in chapter 1 paints a picture of macro-level processes that influence national and local foodscapes. On a micro level, *Black Food Geographies* examines how people move within this context on a day-to-day basis. Although some assert that qualitative inquiry into how people define, consume, and navigate food is vital,[23] research that highlights how Black people shape place in their pursuit of food is often secondary to macro-analyses that focus on the food system as a whole. Margaret Ramirez suggests that a turn toward Black geographic thought disrupts the presumed whiteness of food justice work in communities of color and offers alternative framings for how to understand Black food geographies.[24]

A focus on Black geographies reinscribes Black ways of being, knowing, and doing as essential to understanding place-making, an often neglected aspect of what it means not only to acquire food but also to experience one's community in the process.[25] *Black Food Geographies* focuses on a Black sense of place to center Black humanity rather than solely focusing on suffering and dispossession.[26] This is an effort to examine what is happening rather than simply what is wrong in Black communities, revealing geographies of self-reliance that unfold within spatialized food inequities.

When I use the term "geographies of self-reliance," I am referring to both how residents physically navigate the food landscape—where to shop and how to get there, for example—and more phenomenological concerns: memory, nostalgia, personal and communal priorities, hope, engagements with history, and racialized responsibility. As a theoretical intervention, geographies of self-reliance center Black agency, particularly considering how this agency becomes spatialized within the structural constraints of food inequities. As is evident in qualitative research concerning urban life broadly and urban food access specifically, how the urban poor and the working class survive preoccupies much of the literature, emphasizing how they make ends meet or how inequities continue to block opportunities to provide for themselves.[27] Geographies of self-reliance reveal different yet related experiences, namely, how the everyday lives of residents disrupt the dichotomy between death and survival to reveal how hope and visions for an uncertain future animate decisions on where to shop and who to support, and inspire small-scale food justice work.

Furthermore, self-reliance bridges spatial and sociocultural components of accessing food. Both foodscape and foodways provide frameworks for qualitatively understanding components of food access that are not limited to where grocery stores, supermarkets, and alternative food sources are located. Yet, there is a need to understand the overlap of these two, because residents understand food access through cultural and social lenses that are not divorced from the spatial relations of food resources. Thus, geographies of self-reliance call attention to how spatial, historical, and racial dynamics intersect and insist that Black folks navigate inequities with a creativity that reflects a reliance on self and community. Because of the presumed "nothingness" that is embedded in understandings of so-called food deserts, food justice advocates outside of these neighborhood spaces often overlook or do not see the ways in which residents make "ways out of no way" that are embedded in their own food security and reflect their hopes and desires for their communities more broadly.

Arguably, Black communities' investment in self-reliance as a political and cultural framework for communal uplift has been central to intellectual thought and activist strategizing. Transitions from mass enslavement, migration from the South to the North and West, and integration (albeit limited) into new consumer spheres from which they were once barred prompted questions about how best to meet Black people's needs in a nation in which the rights of full citizenship had yet to be granted. These questions were as fundamentally about space and place as they were about accessing goods. Black residents, many of them living in segregated neighborhoods in urban centers, navigated white supremacy daily, using their segregated neighborhoods as places to build as much institutional capacity to meet their daily needs as possible. Self-reliance became a strategy, a manifesto for building communities that were not wholly reliant on white philanthropy or support.

The question of self-reliance was taken up intellectually. Scholars such as W. E. B. DuBois researched unequal access to housing, food, and employment and theorized ways for Black communities to live as self-sufficiently as possible.[28] DuBois viewed the question of self-sufficiency as a necessity for building healthy, self-sustainable Black communities and as a fundamental blow to an exploitative economic system under which Black intellectual and physical labor were undervalued.[29] Often posited as DuBois's intellectual opposite, Booker T. Washington emphasized technical and agricultural knowledge as means for developing self-reliant communities. For both, self-reliance was a necessary, community-controlled vision and a process toward liberation.

Self-reliance was not solely an intellectual question, however. Black political leaders and activists working toward Black liberation operationalized self-reliance in their community-based work. Fannie Lou Hamer, for example, founded the Freedom Farm Cooperative (FFC) in 1967. Clear in the belief that Black leadership was an imperative for Black liberation, the FFC developed a multifaceted set of social and political programs to address the needs of poor and underemployed Blacks primarily in Mississippi but also as far north as Chicago.[30] Similarly, other activists such as Nannie Helen Burroughs and Anna Julia Cooper (who was also a scholar) argued that without self-reliance, Black communities would not progress. Both were educators and influential women in Washington, D.C., and their visions for a liberated race included a well-rounded, educated Black population—especially Black women—with a diverse skill set. Burroughs founded the National Training School for Women and Girls, where students not only learned reading and writing but were also taught entrepreneurial skills. Indeed, the school itself partially relied on students' skills, as their handmade goods were often sold to help sustain the independent school.

Entrepreneurship as a pathway to self-reliance was not limited to educational institutions like the National Training School for Women and Girls. It was also a foundational place-making strategy central to the development of community identities in the context of anti-Black racism and segregation. Paul Mullins argued that although it raises eyebrows to put entrepreneurship at the center of understanding community identity, the complex network of merchants and consumers that emerged was key to understanding how Black communities have historically functioned, particularly in the first half of the twentieth century.[31]

Improving the "self" as a means of community uplift reflects a form of respectability politics that assumes that performing the right behaviors and having the right education earn rights associated with full citizenship in a racist society, "self" functioning as a proxy for community or representative of the race. This had both positive and negative outcomes, as an individual could be seen as a credit or an embarrassment. It is worth noting that this, too, is a function of living in a racist society in which Black people are hardly given the credit of being an individual—particularly if the outcomes are negative.

However, to dismiss self-reliance as solely about earning the respect of whites obscures the ways in which self-reliance has been woven into the cultural geographies of Black communities across the Diaspora in general, and in the United States in particular. Katherine McKittrick and Clyde Woods argue that "identifying the 'where' of Blackness in positivist terms can reduce Black lives to essential measurable 'facts' rather than presenting communities that have struggled, resisted, and contributed to the production of space."[32] The reduction to "facts," particularly the desire to "bring good food"[33] to Black communities, not only erases Black food geographies, but reinforces the belief that these communities have little or no investment in creating their own place-making strategies toward food self-sufficiency. Scholarship on African American foodways and on-the-ground, Black-led food justice efforts has demonstrated the possibilities and limits of agency and self-reliance within the home and in public spaces. From examinations of kitchens as sites of cultural transmission and self-actualization,[34] to the legacies of the Black Panther Party's organizing to combat hunger as a short-term strategy en route to revolution,[35] to faith-based organizing around food security[36] and current food activism that draws on these histories,[37] self-reliance as a practice of refusal shows up across space and time.

Thus, drawing on intellectual, activist, and scholarly traditions that make self-reliance central to Black liberation, geographies of self-reliance as a theoretical framework situate self-reliance in food consumption and production as a cultural, political, and spatial framework for navigating inequality. Black intellectuals and activists have recognized the usefulness of self-reliance, but so too have residents who have embedded the framework within their everyday practices. The residents I encountered during fieldwork, for example, recognized both the uneven spatial development of their food landscape compared to other neighborhoods and their own agency in transforming that landscape. They ground their analyses and their food place-making strategies in the materiality of Black life, real and imagined connections to historical narratives of successful Black communities, hope and love, and a commitment to "the self" as both individual and communal.

Food justice is fundamentally about racial justice, because in the United States, race and racism not only structure everyday experiences, but also influence the (under)development of neighborhoods and the implementation of policies that disproportionately disenfranchise Black communities. Documenting these inequities and eradicating them is essential as we work toward a more just food system. So, too, is tracing Black food geographies. The Black food geographies included in this book are but a few of the ways Black residents navigate food inequities. These geographies are part of a larger archive, stories that tell the ways inequities shape food consumption by Black residents, but they also bear witness to ways of living and being— Black ways of living and being—that are inseparable from how Black residents understand food access.

Black Food Geographies focuses on practical ways that residents navigate inequity—for example, shopping outside of their neighborhood—but the primary intellectual and theoretical offerings of this book lie in the explorations of how memory, nostalgia, and self-reliance became embedded not only in individuals' experiences with food and community but in the geography of the neighborhood itself and residents' evaluations of it. Black food geographies are influenced by the unequal spatial distribution of grocery stores but are not unilaterally defined by them. I offer geographies of self-reliance as a theoretical frame for understanding how residents were not only concerned with getting to their preferred stores but were also making connections among unequal food distribution, agency of Black people across space and time, and contemporary ways to alter or navigate the unequal landscape. The experiences and stories explored throughout the book were deeply engaged in refusal, whether intentionally or not: refusing to accept the boundedness of neighborhood spaces, refusing to give up hopes that another way is possible, refusing to allow the absence of supermarkets to completely define their foodways. What emerges is a Black sense of place that is both cognizant of discrimination and inequity and reflective of a complex web of possibilities, limitations, and hopes for the neighborhood food system. The stories in the pages to follow are not hypervisible or demanding to be heard. They do, however, require us to *listen*.[38] *Black Food Geographies* is a love letter to and an affirmation of what is possible when we listen to Black people's food stories beyond an all-encompassing narrative of lack.

A Note on Methods

I used four forms of data collection: semistructured interviews, participant observation, archival research, and surveying. During interviews, participants were asked about individual experiences with grocery shopping, cooking, and eating across time, though the interview structure was flexible to accommodate additional directions in which an interviewee wanted to go. They were also asked to discuss their connections to Deanwood, which included accessing food resources as well as what they considered important aspects of their social worlds in the neighborhood. Specifically, I aimed to understand individuals' choices in a broader social context than what was simply on their plates at dinnertime, heeding Robert Sampson's call for observational and qualitative studies that connect people to their spatial contexts.[39] The interviews primarily took place in two locations: Denny's (the only sit-down restaurant in Ward 7) and participants' homes. There were few exceptions to this. In all, I interviewed twenty-five individual participants[40] and one group of eight for this study, ranging from age eighteen to seventy, with the median age being fifty-four. Thirteen of those interviewed individually were women, and the remaining twelve were men.

The second form of data collection was participant observation. Participant observation took place in three main sites: the neighborhood recreation center, Community Market (the subject of chapter 4), and the community garden (the subject of chapter 5). During the first four months of fieldwork, I spent the majority of my time at the recreation center. With after-school activities for school-aged kids, a space specifically for senior citizens, a basketball court, and a pool, it was an ideal place to meet a cross-section of Deanwood residents. The recreation center was the only site I chose for participant observation prior to entering the field. The others were chosen based on informal conversations, interviews, and residents' involvement. Community Market was first mentioned in an interview I conducted with a thirty-year-old participant who had returned to Deanwood the previous year. On a walking tour of the neighborhood, he pointed out a barbershop and Community Market, owned by brothers. Community Market came up again in an interview at Denny's with another long-term resident who grew up in Deanwood. After that, I visited the store for the first time. My first encounter with Mr. Jones, the store owner, is described in chapter 4.

Aside from Community Market, corner stores and small markets are noticeably absent in this book, with the exception of discussions of how Community Market functioned in the neighborhood vis-à-vis comparisons to other stores. There is a reason for this. Despite the attention given to corner stores in food access literature, they did not figure prominently in residents' consumption patterns. Only one resident spoke about making a conscious choice between going to a corner store or the nearest supermarket. That is discussed in detail in chapter 2. There may be several reasons why corner stores were inconsequential for the majority of my participants. First, participants almost unanimously considered the nearby Safeway to be subpar, but all shopped there at some point, even if the purchases they made on those occasions were minimal or strategic. Second, all of my research participants—even those who did not own their own transportation—had figured out strategies for procuring groceries that did not require depending on corner stores and small markets. A third and final reason relates to Community Market itself. None of my participants relied on corner stores or small markets for their shopping, but several of them considered Community Market to be distinct from corner stores. Continuously owned and operated by the same family, Community Market itself represented the possibilities of self-reliance.

I began participant observation at the community garden at a public housing complex in October 2013 after being in contact with the primary gardener for nearly a year. Over the course of seven months, I attended and participated in two planting events, shadowed the primary gardener during planting and weeding, and observed kids' involvement in the daily maintenance of the garden. Five of the research participants I interviewed were affiliated with the garden. Related to observing the garden was the community center in the complex. The center served as a central meeting location as well as the home for several social service agencies in the projects. Dating back to 1976, the center was opened as a resource for community members and continued to serve in that capacity during my fieldwork. Here, I met with two members of the resident council and the primary gardener, and observed a workshop on healthy eating and cooking.

In addition to the main sites, I visited and observed the closest Safeway, which was subject to much critique in almost all the interviews. I also observed the neighborhood and residents more informally by walking the streets, volunteering and participating at the local community center, and attending neighborhood association meetings that I was welcomed to join by the president of the citizens' association.

The third form of data collection was archival research. Deanwood has little written, published history. Much of what I knew about the neighborhood's history I learned from elders in the community. I used archival research to confirm and supplement residents' stories. The Historical Society of Washington, D.C., proved to be a great source of maps documenting how Deanwood grew and changed in the first half of the twentieth century. The George Washington University Library houses Ruth Ann Overbeck's papers, another critical source of data for this project. Overbeck was a local historian who spent much of her career documenting D.C. neighborhoods. Her papers include twenty oral history interviews with Deanwood residents, an archaeological assessment of Deanwood, and home and business directories. The participants interviewed as part of Overbeck's project ranged from age seventy to age eighty-six in 1987. Of those whose gender was specified, eleven respondents were women and eight were men. Eighteen of the respondents owned their homes, and only two rented. All had been married at least once, and seven were widowed at the time of interview. Eighteen of the respondents were at least high school graduates, seven had completed four years of college, and one had completed more than four years of college. Chapter 1 draws heavily from the sources included in Overbeck's papers.

In 2016, I, along with a collaborator from the neighborhood I had met several years prior, conducted a survey of Ward 7 residents. The survey had a dual purpose. First, for the community, the intent was for the collected data to be used to discuss food access and plan a way forward. At the time, there were several disparate conversations about improving access for Ward 7 residents. The hope was that this data would put some numbers behind the anecdotal experiences that we all knew were true but were not always heard by those in power. Second, I wanted to broaden the understanding of food access in Ward 7 by including additional neighborhoods. One hundred one participants began the survey, and eighty-seven completed it. As discussed in chapter 2, the survey revealed trends in residents' shopping preferences and critiques of Safeway. The data is also helpful for situating Deanwood within a broader geographic and social landscape.

From Middle School Class to Food Access Research

I often tell people that teaching middle school changed the course of my life and career. In the two years prior to entering graduate school, I taught a group of dynamic and curious Black girls at Coretta Scott King Young Women's Leadership Academy, a public single-gender school in Atlanta, Georgia. Having grown up in rural East Texas, I was still relatively new to cities, their organizational structures, and the specific ways inequities shape and unfold within them. One day, I took two students to get sports physicals so they could join the track team. After a long wait and the completed exams, it was nearing dinnertime, so I offered to feed them before taking them home.

A routine trip to my neighborhood supermarket was out of the ordinary for them. Imagine two Black girls who were normally loud and giggly sticking closely to me, silently observing the space. When we got to my house so that I could make dinner, one of them asked, "Why is your store so nice?" There were questions about the types of fruits and vegetables available and comments about how there was not anything "that nice" in their neighborhood. Their neighborhood was a mere 3.9 miles from where I lived. We talked a lot that night, and I was not satisfied with my own naïveté and lack of knowledge about food access. Their questions became my questions, their lives the inspiration for conducting research that would ultimately become this book.

In 2012, I entered the field to start the research that would become this book. During fieldwork, I did not live in Deanwood. I lived about twenty minutes away in Takoma Park, Maryland. I commuted back and forth to Deanwood nearly every day to visit the recreation center, to interview participants, and to hang out. While I did not live in the neighborhood, living in the D.C. metro area afforded me both proximity and mobility to spend ample amounts of time there. To my knowledge, not living in the neighborhood did not hinder the project's development. Generally, people were willing and eager to learn more about my research and me. Over time, people would shout greetings to me, acknowledging my presence when I walked down the street.

In the field, I was a Black feminist anthropologist, coming in and out of a neighborhood where I did not live, but one for which I developed a deep affinity. I gained entry into the neighborhood through volunteering at the recreation center. After teaching middle school, I felt comfortable hanging out with and tutoring children. I called the recreation center to inquire about being a tutor and was welcomed enthusiastically. Being a Black woman helped facilitate my entry into the recreation center (where the staff and patrons are almost entirely Black) and provided some common ground for myself and my research participants. There were many moments, though, when I did not meet the expectations that are sometimes affixed to racial solidarity, especially when it came to having conversations around gender, sexuality, deservedness, and the value of "hard work." These were some of the toughest conversations, and I am not sure I always handled them well. But no one turned me away when I vehemently disagreed or expressed discomfort. Instead, they generally remained interested in my work, and when I'd come around, some would ask something like, "How's that book you're writing?"

At the recreation center, I was upfront about my studies, and I was almost immediately bombarded with requests to teach "healthy eating" skills, something that made me uncomfortable, because one of the things I feel strongly about is how African Americans and other people of color are often reduced to bodies that need to be regulated and changed. I awkwardly consented to doing some things—like making smoothies with the kids—and avoided committing to others. Ironically, though, these requests helped me take a critical look at what I thought about the connections between eating and health in African American communities. I began to think about the myths and realities of soul food, the origins of gardening, and the ways Black folks empower themselves to make decisions about their eating and health in the context of food inequities.

Some people, like Mr. Johnson, were eager to talk. Others were confused about what I was there to do. Why did I want to talk about food and where they shopped? Could I teach the children at the local recreation center about healthy eating? Would my research lead to a new supermarket or grocery store in the area? These questions were not always easy to answer, but they were influential, as they, in some cases painfully, helped me see just how deeply entrenched the idea that Black people need fixing is in our discourses about improving access and healthy eating. When asked questions about if I was there to help people eat better, I learned to say, "I am not here to tell you what is healthy and what is not or to tell you what you should buy. I am here to learn from you and to always advocate for your right to have choices and live the life you want to live." Ultimately, the uncomfortable and awkward conversations, the familiarity and trust that developed over time, and the generosity that was extended to me were indispensable for the development of *Black Food Geographies*. Where I, theory, or method fell short or faltered, Deanwood residents offered care and insight that you will read throughout these pages.

Summary of Chapters

Black Food Geographies explores Black residents' experiences with and meanings of food institutions in Deanwood specifically and Washington, D.C., more broadly. Chapter 1, "Come to Think of It, We Were Pretty Self-Sufficient: Race, Segregation, and Food Access in Historical Context," places food access in historical context, tracing the development of Washington, D.C.'s food system in the twentieth century. This chapter explores Deanwood's particular food system, highlighting how self-reliance and race shaped the neighborhood and the challenges of maintaining a self-contained neighborhood within the context of the rise and subsequent decline of supermarkets in the poorest and Blackest areas of Washington, D.C.

Focusing on the closest supermarket as a site for understanding residents' critiques of their food environment and their preferences, chapter 2, "There Ain't Nothing in Deanwood: Navigating Nothingness and the *Un*Safeway," explores how residents frame, use, and avoid Safeway. First, I examine the many considerations at the heart of grocery shopping: time, money, stores' reputation, transportation, and preferences. Second, I examine how these considerations are connected to socioeconomic status, demonstrating the heterogeneity present in the neighborhood. Chapter 3, "What Is Our Culture? I Don't Even Know: Nostalgia and Memory in Evaluations of Food

Access," explores how memories of and storytelling about the past figure into how residents understand present-day food inequities. The chapter examines how race, gender, and class (and to an extent age) factor into how residents frame the problem of food access and narratives of responsibility.

Chapter 4, "He's Had That Store for Years: The Historical and Symbolic Value of Community Market," examines Community Market as a hopeful symbol of racial progress and self-reliance. Placed within the historical context outlined in chapter 1 and the contemporary realities of low food access exhibited in chapter 2, I examine the paradox of residents exhibiting pride in the store while at the same time not shopping there on a regular basis. I also explore the role the second-generation owner, Mr. Jones, plays in the community at large, making the argument that the position of authority that many residents claim he has is in part due to the longevity of the store, even in the face of gentrification. Chapter 5, "We Will Not Perish; We Will Flourish: Community Gardening, Self-Reliance, and Refusal," focuses on the community garden at a public housing complex. In this chapter, I highlight the ways this garden operates within a framework concerned with providing fresh fruits and vegetables to low-income residents while at the same time leveraging the garden as a site of resistance in response to the failures of public housing.

Lastly, the concluding chapter, "Black Lives and Black Food Futures," reflects on intersecting oppressions and what this means in the context of food justice activism and research. It turns to considering the ways participants highlighted in this book and contemporary Black-led food movements are creating blueprints for Black food futures—ones in which residents have more food options that reflect values important to Black place-making and community building.

CHAPTER ONE

Come to Think of It,
We Were Pretty Self-Sufficient

Race, Segregation, and Food Access
in Historical Context

When I began fieldwork, D.C. residents and visitors alike asked, "Where is Deanwood?" Located in upper northeast Washington, D.C., Deanwood is tucked along Division and Eastern Avenues, dividing lines between the District and Prince George's County, Maryland. Nannie Helen Burroughs Avenue and the Anacostia Freeway complete the official boundaries used for census purposes, though these boundaries expand or contract, depending on who you ask and their social or historical ties to the neighborhood.[1] The small-town feel struck me almost immediately on my first visit. Single-family brick and wood-framed homes, sizeable front and back yards, and the protectiveness of residents toward their neighborhood reminded me of rural East Texas where I grew up.

The main street that runs through the heart of the neighborhood had all the features typically associated with an unhealthy food environment: two small corner stores less than a half mile from each other, a liquor store, a carryout, and an old, abandoned soul food restaurant. People—mostly women—got on and off buses with plastic Safeway bags as they traveled to and from the closest supermarket, on Minnesota Avenue. Signs of urban disinvestment, the systematic loss of grocery stores, and middle-class flight were visible. These are what my eyes were trained to look for as a food systems researcher. They told stories I had become familiar with and would become even more so: stories of a struggling food environment that needed new life breathed into it. When I began conducting formal interviews, I usually asked residents to begin wherever they liked. Some began with memories. Others began with their shopping practices. Many, however, paused before beginning with a narrative that is all too familiar—one in which "nothingness" is evoked as a definitive, unchanging truth about the neighborhood. Beyond the surface, though, were other stories to be heard. While the neighborhood's immediately visible physical condition hardly painted a picture of a self-reliant community that once met most of residents' needs, residents' memories, stories, and the archives said otherwise. Despite the pervasive "nothingness" that many residents used as a starting point in their interviews, very few ended there as past, present, and future intertwined to reveal nuances in how residents witnessed, remembered, or experienced the changing food system.

This chapter begins with an examination of how Deanwood became a "self-reliant" community, emphasizing food's role in connecting residents to the South, to each other, and to various strategies used to build and maintain community, despite persisting racial inequities. I go on to examine the displacement of small grocery stores in the neighborhood—many of which were Jewish-owned—during the shift toward supermarkets as preferred food retailers. Lastly, I end with where many narratives begin, with an examination of how the systematic decline of supermarkets shaped the food landscape of Deanwood and Washington, D.C.

The Early Makings of a Self-Reliant Community

What is now known as Deanwood was once farmland worked by enslaved Black people. Ninian Beall, a white farmer, initially acquired it as part of a land grant in 1703.[2] Ownership changed hands multiple times, but by 1833 Levi Sheriff, another white farmer, purchased it. When he died, Sheriff's three daughters subdivided the land in 1871 after realizing that the decline the family farm underwent during the Civil War was likely irreversible.[3]

When the sisters developed these subdivisions, it is likely they assumed that white families would be attracted to the newly built homes, the expansive landscape, and the railway that ran through Deanwood from Bladensburg, Maryland, to a Potomac River wharf. By 1873, however, only two plots of land had sold, for a total of $50.[4] In 1874, the next buyer purchased one of the subdivisions, offering the sisters two plots in the city center in exchange. Reverend John H. W. Burley, who purchased the subdivision, was the first African American on record to purchase land in the Deanwood area, setting a precedent for Black landownership in the community.

Archival records between 1874 and the turn of the twentieth century are unclear concerning how African Americans heard of Deanwood or why they chose to move there. It is likely that word of mouth traveled routes similar to those followed by the people who made up what we call the Great Migration—throngs of Black people looking for opportunities in urban centers around the country. What is clear, however, is that Black residents established institutions that were key to community sustainability. Between

1880 and 1886, residents built Contee African Methodist Episcopal Zion Church and the Burrville School, the first to serve African American students in the greater Deanwood community. In 1909, Nannie Helen Burroughs opened the National Training School for Women and Girls. The school operated on three principles: Bible, bath, and broom. In its first twenty-five years, the National Training School for Women and Girls matriculated over 2,000 girls and women from across the United States, the Caribbean, and African nations.[5] By 1926, at least six additional churches were built, several along the main thoroughfare that would later be named Sheriff Road after one of the white slaveholding farmers who originally owned land where Deanwood sits.

The mass exodus of African Americans from southern cities during the Great Migration left its mark on D.C. generally and Deanwood specifically. In 1920, Washington, D.C.'s Black population was 110,000.[6] Ten years later, that number had grown to 132,000, with a great majority of new Washingtonians hailing from Virginia, North Carolina, and South Carolina, where the agricultural system had begun to decline after World War I.[7] These migration trends were consistent in Deanwood. Among the residents included in an oral history project conducted by D.C. historian Ruth Ann Overbeck, eight out of twenty participants or their families had migrated to Deanwood from other southern states such as Virginia, North Carolina, and South Carolina. Others moved there from other parts of the city and did not detail if they had origins elsewhere.[8] Their reasons for choosing Deanwood varied. Some families sought Deanwood at the encouragement of friends or relatives who already lived there. Others came in search of educational opportunities for their children and thought Deanwood would provide a better environment. Still others were seeking more progressive racial and economic climates than what they experienced in their home states. Though migrants could not escape the anti-Blackness that created little or no access to schooling and a sharecropping system in the South that amounted to another form of bondage, urban centers like Washington, D.C. — combined with the talents they brought with them — gave them hope for creating better futures for themselves and their children.

While there were variations in economic stability, many early Deanwood residents built or purchased homes, which they saw as integral to upward mobility. Ninety percent of those interviewed by Overbeck in 1987 owned their homes, which they acquired through a direct purchase, receivership from parents, transfer from grandparents or other relatives, or marriage. Homeownership was one outcome of a larger commitment to creating model, sustainable communities. In the pursuit of homeownership, early Deanwood residents brought a desire for better lives that was steeped in self-reliance and resilience. Racial uplift ideologies through which residents created community cohesion and navigated the physical, social, and economic constraints of racism were integral to the development of Black neighborhoods across the United States. Kevin Gaines argued that meanings of racial uplift primarily fell into two categories: (1) emphasizing education as key to liberation, and (2) elevating "self-help, racial solidarity, temperance, thrift, chastity, social purity, patriarchal authority, and the accumulation of wealth" as mechanisms through which to develop well-rounded people and create safe, stable communities that would push back against the belief that African Americans were inferior to whites.[9] Commonly referred to as respectability politics, these ideologies and the practices that resulted from them were not simply about creating healthy, safe communities. Nonwhite and immigrant communities in the United States often responded to white supremacy by performing behaviors that were associated with being cultured, well-mannered, and educated. While they often very well knew and recognized that anti-Blackness influenced and structured their neighborhoods and access to resources, many early twentieth-century nonwhite and immigrant communities chose to not openly agitate white people or the structures they created as a strategy for survival, even as others fought openly and fiercely for equality and justice.

In D.C., communities that formed reflected Black people's commitments to surviving in spite of white supremacy. Compared to a neighborhood like Shaw, which had emerged as a center of Black culture and intellectual life in D.C.,[10] Deanwood seemed like the backwoods. Established by freedmen on the outskirts of Washington City in the nineteenth century, Shaw was home to several prominent African Americans and to some of the most prestigious African American institutions: Howard University, the Whitlaw Hotel, Industrial Savings Bank, and Freedmen's Hospital.[11] Though it had the only amusement park for Black residents in the early twentieth century and was well connected to railways, Deanwood neither looked nor felt as developed as its counterpart. Deanwood, east of the Anacostia River, was considered by other Washingtonians as distinct from "the city" of Washington because of its relative physical and social isolation from the African American epicenters.[12] City services were slower. Roads were not paved until well into the 1950s, and even then, some residents still did not have indoor plumbing. A hand-drawn map from 1948 described Deanwood as "mainly a Negro residential area" that, in spite of nicely kept homes, displayed "the usual

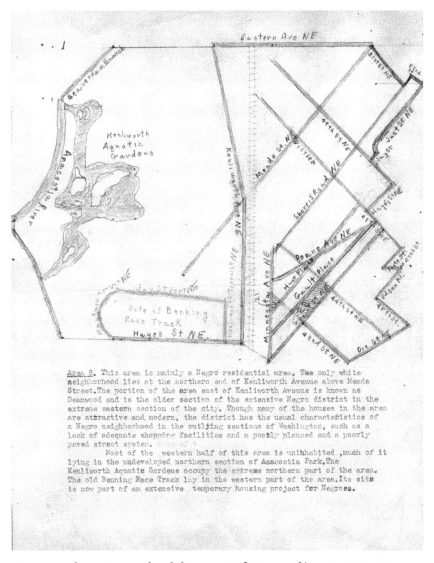

Area 8. This area is mainly a Negro residential area. The only white neighborhood lies at the northern end of Kenilworth Avenue above Meade Street. The portion of the area east of Kenilworth Avenue is known as Deanwood and is the older section of the extensive Negro district in the extreme eastern section of the city. Though many of the houses in the area are attractive and modern, the district has the usual characteristics of a Negro neighborhood in the outlying sections of Washington, such as a lack of adequate shopping facilities and a poorly planned and a poorly paved street system.

Most of the western half of this area is uninhabited, much of it lying in the undeveloped northern section of Anacostia Park. The Kenilworth Aquatic Gardens occupy the extreme northern part of the area. The old Benning Race Track lay in the western part of the area. Its site is now part of an extensive temporary housing project for Negroes.

FIGURE 1 John P. Wymer's hand-drawn map of Deanwood in 1948. WY 0397M.08, John P. Wymer Photograph Collection, Historical Society of Washington, D.C.

characteristics of a Negro neighborhood in the outlying sections of Washington, such as a lack of adequate shopping facilities and a poorly planned and poorly paved street system."[13] The map and the language used to describe the area illustrate the racial segregation that, by the time the map was drawn, was an expected and normal part of residential — and to some extent commercial — life for those who lived in Deanwood (see figure 1).

Yet, it should not be assumed that people were less industrious than their counterparts in parts of D.C. that had better infrastructure. Indeed, they were creating community and making lives. The combination of people who settled there—migrants from the South, skilled craftsmen, and entrepreneurs—worked to create a community that met most of residents' needs, despite the challenges presented by racism, physical isolation, and vastly undeveloped tracts of land.

Growing Food

Owning land and homes provided the space for farming and gardening, which were integral to the growth and development of Deanwood in the first half of the twentieth century. For example, Vincent Bunch reported that around 1923, his parents sold the land they owned in South Carolina, packed up their lives, and moved to the nation's capital. Although they had owned their land in South Carolina, they were still hoping D.C. was a great place to raise children, to make more money, and to not have to farm. Vincent's father had been an industrial education teacher after he finished college but sought other employment when they moved to D.C., because "back in those days Pullman [porters] seem[ed] like they made a little bit more money. He could make more money being a Pullman than he could teaching school in little southern schools."[14] When they arrived, Vincent's parents and their firstborn son lived with family until they were able to purchase the materials needed to build their home in Deanwood:

> Yes, I was born in Deanwood. My parents came from another state, but when they first came, my dad . . . they lived with my aunt in town until he got squared away with his house out here. At the same time, they were building it because a good portion of the lumber that the house was built with, he built it, he had it shipped from South Carolina. I can't say exactly when he started to build it or when he got finished. You see, back [then], he was still running on the road. He would come to town. He would work on [the house]. So, it wasn't like a house that went straight through from start to finish because I think even our kitchen was an addition. It was a lot of work.[15]

Within two years of arriving in Washington, D.C., the family's home was finished, and they welcomed another son, Vincent, who would later be interviewed about living and shopping in Deanwood in its early formation as a Black enclave.

Many early Deanwood residents like Vincent's parents had complex relationships with the Deep South and farming. On one hand, they left in search of something better than lifelong farming, which often had to be supplemented with other work. For those who migrated from states in the Deep South in particular, farming was emblematic of the continued subjugation of African Americans who were unfairly cheated out of money, their labor, or produce. On the other hand, the skills they learned as farmers were used to cultivate a multifaceted foodscape in Deanwood that included gardens, small farms, and independently owned general stores that primarily sold dry goods, some freshly slaughtered meats, and household items needed to meet daily needs. Despite the pull away from the Deep South and the Black agrarianism that largely built its economy, the same skills that were associated with subjugation were used as liberation tools, as early residents used them to develop individual and communal self-sufficiency.

Vincent was interviewed in 1987 about life in Deanwood in the 1930s and 1940s. At the time of his interview, he was a sixty-two-year-old married Deanwood resident who had recently retired from the Interior Department, where he had worked as a cartographer. In his interview, he reflected on several aspects of the food environment, which included the strategies his parents employed to meet their food needs:

> See my father bought six lots. The house set on two lots, there were two on this side of the house and two on the other side! And two of the lots are still there. We planted everything . . . uh corn, sweet potatoes, uh peanuts, greens and stuff like that. Squash, peppers and tomatoes. We had seven peach trees, two apple trees and one plum tree that didn't bear too much . . . and a cherry tree. And there was a pecan tree. The pecan tree is still there . . . years back when my mother brought that tree up, she brought it up from South Carolina, and we planted it. We could get . . . I'd say maybe from two or three shoeboxes full! Now the squirrels came in and got them. Come to think about it, we were pretty self-sufficient . . . our food needs.[16]

Above all else, owning land was the basis on which Vincent's parents planned not only where they would live, but also what they would eat. Working the land became part of everyday practice as residents used food production as a means to both resist the subjugation associated with the Deep South and to plant roots that connected their D.C. experiences with their former homes. Rather than repudiating their southernness, they resisted the "backwardness" associated with the South through their land cultivating skills and ingenuity. Vincent's narrative suggests that not only did his parents create and maintain these foodways, but they also planned for them, buying six lots instead of just the two necessary for their home. This was not atypical, as most African Americans in the Deep South and those who migrated north attempted to maintain at least small gardens to be self-sufficient.[17] The South showed up in their gardens, in their stores, and in the self-reliance strategies they cultivated to created new lives in Deanwood.

Selling produce from homes or carts and wagons was part of Deanwood's local economy until the early 1950s. Julia Parks noted, "Mothers were reported to have prepared and marketed foodstuffs from their homes until licensing became a requirement. At least two fathers of the respondents were remembered as selling their produce from carts within the community, out of their homes, and at the Florida Ave. Market as well."[18] Those fathers were known by most as hucksters. Though many of the early residents were educated, growing and selling food was one way to either make a living or supplement their income. Individual-level economies — as represented by the hucksters — were supported by community buy-in and support.[19] Deanwood provided a viable market that was invested in both the needs of their individual families and the success of the hucksters, who were often their neighbors. Allison, a sixty-eight-year-old Deanwood resident, remembered her family's engagement with the hucksters, joking that she had forgotten about them, probably because her ex-boyfriend from her younger days was a huckster who came through the neighborhood selling whiting from boxes. When he would come down their street selling fish, her mother would say, "There goes your huckster," as she tried to avoid him. She recalled: "They would come through on the wagons. They would bring fish here. They brought vegetables, watermelon . . . I mean, especially before the Safeway and of course, when the Safeway came through that sort of cut into their . . . But yeah, I had forgot about the hucksters . . . The vendors who would come through with their horses . . . yeah I know all about the hucksters. Yeah, the vendors that would come through with their horses and eventually, I think, there probably were trucks that came through." Allison illustrates both the business and the interpersonal aspects of the practice. Supporting local businesses not only supplemented individual families' food production, but also reinforced the belief that self-reliance was as much about communal survival as it was about individual gain.[20] Her narrative also foreshadows forces that disrupted self-reliance: corporate growth in food production and perceived modernity. The tensions produced by these changes — the results of which are still manifesting in the contemporary landscape—are the conditions that past and present residents found themselves navigating. Changes in the food system were not solely evident in consumer behavior. They also influenced community relationships, putting Black residents in a position to redefine what it meant to "buy Black." What may have been an everyday part of the food landscape prior to widespread changes became more of a challenge. As pointed out in Allison's narrative, supermarkets challenged community-based practices such as huckstering. The convenience and variety offered by these larger stores created a food environment in which hucksters could not compete. Though supermarkets were only just beginning to gain traction in the 1940s and 1950s as the preferred venue for obtaining groceries, early evidence of the damage they caused in neighborhoods—and by extension in social relationships—is present in Allison's narrative.

Trading and bartering formed part of the informal economy in Deanwood, and to residents were integral to economic sustainability, considering the myriad ways they were marginalized in formal economic sectors. For my research participants who were over sixty-five and had grown up in Deanwood, memories of their parents' gardens were key components of their reflections on food acquisition. Reflecting on her mother's garden, nearly life-long Deanwood resident Anne placed it within a context that highlighted the role of food production in community cohesion:

> I remember my mother growing squash, cucumbers, tomatoes, corn. I think we might have had some . . . I'm not sure about the corn. I'm not going to swear by the corn, though. We did have a peach tree. And the kids would steal the peaches off the tree. But what was ever left, she made a peach wine from them. Yeah, I remember that in the basement, in fact . . . I'm trying to think where. Is it on the front porch or did I take it downstairs? One of the original pots that she used to make the peach wine in. Yeah, we were really self-contained and people would trade things. "Okay, who wants something?" . . . "I have some corn over here, I have extra corn." . . . or you know, if it's a dozen and you don't need the whole dozen.

Anthropological research in predominantly Black communities has noted the importance of trading and bartering not only as strategies to meet individual needs but also as important forms of social and cultural capital through which community cohesion was built.[21] In the contemporary food landscape, the loss of this bartering and exchange is what residents pointed to as an indication that the social fabric of the neighborhood had shifted. This loss was not only about acquiring food but also, as explored in subsequent chapters, served as a litmus test for how residents evaluated community cohesion.

Small Grocers

In addition to producing food for family consumption and selling it, other entrepreneurial pursuits were a foundational component of Deanwood's early development. Though many African Americans in D.C. were able to obtain government employment, many others explored entrepreneurship in their segregated neighborhoods. It provided an opportunity for African American business owners to both serve their neighborhoods and resist racist structures that constrained physical, economic, and social mobility. The capital generated contributed to the economic and social vitality of these neighborhoods.[22] Residents in Deanwood were no different. Overbeck and colleagues noted that Black businesses were the crux of community economic development in Deanwood:

> Between 1907 and 1945, Deanwood had a wide variety and number of small businesses owned and operated by black persons. About a dozen types of businesses were reported. These included small groceries, pharmacies, coal and ice services, a shoe repair, eating and food services, a combined real estate and grocery, funeral parlors, a materials transport business and bus service, cleaners and an oil company. In addition, large scale and small scale building and building related crafts were carried out commercially . . . Crafts such as electrical, plumbing, cement finishing and stone making were typically carried out as both a business and as community activity.[23]

Overbeck's analysis suggests that the self-reliance ethos that undergirded much of Deanwood's development was as much about community-building and community success as it was about individuals' thriving. Steven Gregory illustrated that community-building and community success were central to the development of predominantly Black communities, if for no other reason than that equal protection under the law was not a reality. The political power, social networks, and skills that were shared were invaluable in terms of creating a thriving neighborhood.[24]

Some of the earliest stores between 1900 and 1930 were food stores, which supplemented individual families' food production. In her description of

Black-owned businesses, Parks noted, "It is likely that food stores emerged first and in connection with individuals selling surplus food stuffs raised on small 'farm type land.'"[25] There was, however, a disconnect between Black-owned food stores and what residents described as central to their shopping practices. Seven Black-owned food stores were identified during the interviews with Overbeck, but none of the twenty respondents included any commentary on shopping at these stores for their daily food needs. Respondents' explicit commentary about Black-owned food stores was scant. Instead, Jewish-owned and -operated stores were a central theme in their oral histories (see map 1). While Black-owned food stores developed before the arrival of Jewish-owned stores, a distinct difference was that Black-owned stores were more likely to occupy renovated homes, whereas Jewish-owned businesses were constructed as commercial properties.[26] This potentially explains why in Overbeck's oral history interviews, Black-owned grocery stores were more likely to be identified by the name of the store owner rather than by a formal store name. It is possible that the type of physical space that stores occupied and the products they could hold factored into how residents conceptualized the stores.[27]

Although Jewish immigrants did not flock to Washington, D.C., in as large numbers as they did to cities like New York, the District had a sizeable Jewish population that reached 100,000 by 1918.[28] Seeking jobs in factories that did not require the use of much English was a defining characteristic among Jewish immigrants overall but was not necessarily true of those who came to D.C. Many of those who migrated to D.C. had already been living in the United States, had knowledge and experience navigating U.S. race relations and politics, and favored entrepreneurship over industrial work.[29] Mom-and-pop grocery stores were among the most successful entrepreneurial pursuits.

Jewish families purchased property, opened grocery stores, and set up living space either above or behind their stores, sometimes working seven days a week.[30] They were spurred by the ideals of upward mobility, not unlike Black migrants who saw education, entrepreneurship, and hard work as important tools in their children's pursuit of stable, middle-class lives. In both cases, the desire for upward mobility was two-pronged: a desire for greater wealth and comfort for future generations and a marked response or reaction to the racist, oppressive systems in the United States that discriminated against each group in varying ways. The racial hierarchy that marked Jews as "not quite white enough" thrived on the sometimes precarious relationship between them and African Americans.[31] By the end of the 1920s, the

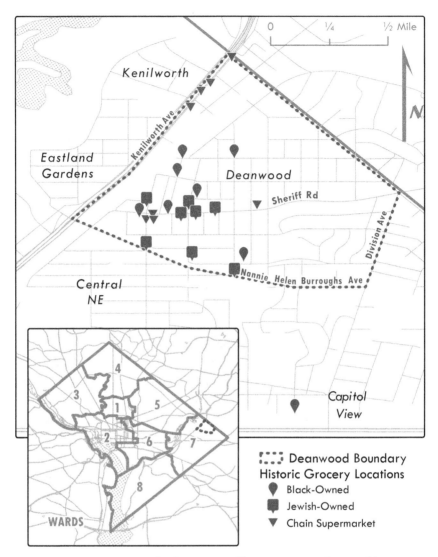

MAP 1 Grocery stores operating in Deanwood between 1925 and 1960. This map was created based on stores that were reported in the Overbeck oral history interviews and those collected in an online database called Groceteria. Groceteria is a website dedicated to exploring the history of supermarkets in urban areas. As part of the website, the author includes a database of supermarkets opened in Washington, D.C., between 1925 and 1975. A detailed methodology is included on the site. For a complete list of store openings in Washington, D.C., visit http://www .groceteria.com/place/washington-dc/chain-supermarkets-in-washington-dc-1925 -1975/. Map courtesy of Emeline Renz (@mapgrrl).

only non-Blacks who lived in Deanwood were the Jewish store owners, adding to the complex entrepreneurship and self-reliance narrative upon which Deanwood was founded.

Respondents in Overbeck's oral history of Deanwood identified eight Jewish-owned grocery stores, many of which were part of the District Grocery Store (DGS) cooperative. Begun in 1922 by twelve Jewish store owners who pooled their resources to buy directly from manufacturers, DGS comprised over 300 stores in the Washington, D.C., area at its peak.[32] In a 1963 article in the *Washington Post* titled "Small Stores Thrive through Cooperation," William Raspberry quoted Henry Noon, then president of the DGS collective: "Our wholesale operation is a terrific thing for small merchants . . . because of our volume buying and our connection with Eastern Retail Grocers (a division of Cooperative Food Distributors of America) we are able to keep our wholesale prices so low that our merchants can often undersell the chains on such perishables as meats and produce."[33] Collective buying power yielded greater products at better prices, which resulted in consistent, repeat clientele for DGS stores in Deanwood and a distinctiveness from Black-owned grocery stores.

One of the defining characteristics of the Jewish-owned stores was the credit system, which allowed residents to charge their groceries and settle their bills at the end of each month. One resident recalled, "Most of the people paid cash, but I know there was a [Jewish] store on the corner from me that had a little book. And you could buy on credit, and he'd write in the little book, and they would pay for their purchases by the month . . . their relations with black people were very amiable. Yeah they were nice! They remembered the people too! The Black people [*sic*] felt like they were accepted."[34] Noticeably, she remarked that the Black people felt "accepted," highlighting both the material realities and the irony of segregation. In this segregated neighborhood, where Black residents were the overwhelming majority, being accepted by Jewish store owners stood out as a phenomenon to comment on. The resident also points out the personalized aspects of shopping at the store. Not only were the store owners nice, but they also remembered people, which potentially translated into repeat clientele, since relationships were key the neighborhood grocery model.[35] Dorothy M. Roberts offered a similar perspective:

Well we did [our shopping] most at Fisher's there at 46th and Sheriff Road, cause we had to come up from where we lived down there. And then in later years, we shopped at the store that was at 44th and Sheriff

Road. I can't think of his name now, he was Jewish. Then they had a Safeway at 44th and Sheriff Road and we shopped in there . . . And then we had the store right here at the corner. It was a DGS Store, and we shopped there. And they were very good to the blacks. Because they did not allow them to, they did not go hungry, let me put it that way. Because they would uh, definitely let you have food until payday. And they had good food, don't kid yourself! Those [District Grocery Stores], they had good meats if nothing else![36]

Her commentary highlights her perceptions of the merit of the credit system: "they did not go hungry," "they" being families who relied on the system to get by until payday. In her words, the store owners demonstrated being "very good to blacks" through the credit system, thereby solidifying themselves not only as store owners, but also as productive citizens and contributors in the neighborhood.

However, relationships between store owners and residents were not always amicable or perceived as fair. Participants also speculated that those who used the credit system were sometimes cheated out of their money. Dorothy Slaughter Dixon described her experience at a Jewish-owned store:

Once in a while, I went to the [Jewish-owned] stores, but I didn't like that much. Most of the people just ran a book as they called it and they would charge them on anything they felt like. And nearly everybody around here was on the book . . . some of them would leave the book in the store, and I caught the old white woman, the [one] up at the store. When the little girl came in and she had . . . she kept the books there . . . some would leave the book there . . . and she would leave the spaces in between the amounts. She wouldn't put down what they had bought, she'd put the figures down they had bought. And I was standing there looking, she was waiting on the little girl, and she had these empty spaces, and while she was talking she just filled them in, putting extra money in! And the people will come to pay the bill and they would have a great big bill! But I mean, they were as crooked as a ram's horn! So I didn't . . . I used to go in there once in a while.[37]

Similarly, Emily Marin also suspected residents were cheated out of money:

Well, I don't know about credit, because I always paid cash for whatever I got, even the [Jewish owner] on the corner didn't like me cause I gave him hell about it. You see he used to mark up things on people and I went up there one day and [he was] marking up somebody's by putting a piece of meat and putting it on the scale and making it heavy. So I never bought anything from him but bread and milk. And I only bought that when I ran out, you know cause I got my milk from the dairy.[38]

Collectively, the two commentaries illustrate the nuances of shopping in Deanwood, particularly as it relates to race, class, and negotiating where to shop. Of the twenty participants in Overbeck's study, none indicated that Black-owned grocery stores kept books or cheated shoppers. However, the ability to charge food items was a favored strategy among those who had limited cash while trying to make ends meet. Dorothy Slaughter Dixon's commentary suggests that residents knew that their end-of-the-month bills were higher than they were supposed to be, but given the precariousness of financial situations for many residents, they, unlike Dorenthia, who would choose to go "every once in a while," may not have had many options.

Emily Marin's commentary, just like Dorothy's, suggests that she based her shopping practices in part based on what she witnessed in one of the Jewish-owned stores. Although she pointed out that she did not buy groceries on credit, it is unclear whether or not "marking up" happened in a way similar way to that described by Dorenthia. However, what is clear is that Emily demonstrates a degree of negotiation. She implies that she would not buy anything that required weighing, but she would buy prepackaged staples such as bread and milk, which effectively keeps the option open for emergencies while also displaying a degree of moral indignation toward the store owner. This speaks to her agency as a shopper, but it also speaks to the landscape of choice in the neighborhood. With a number of stores in the neighborhood, Marin could afford to not be liked by this particular storeowner. The landscape of choice that characterized early Deanwood, however, would change as demographics shifted and supermarkets became the standard for food procurement.

Transitioning to Supermarkets: The Makings of the Grocery Gap in Washington, D.C.

Gardens, small farms, and neighborhood grocers may have characterized the early twentieth century, but it is the supermarket that emerged as the quintessential component of the national and local food system, so much so that narratives around fixing broken food systems often begin with the supermarket—not the ways people historically created local foodways.

In the 1930s, the largest grocery stores averaged between 6,000 and 8,000 square feet. By the 1960s, supermarkets were as large as 60,000 to 80,000 square feet.[39] The structural changes that accompanied supermarkets have had lasting effects on national and local levels. Even though Henry Noon boasted that the DGS was thriving as late as 1963, the cooperative dissolved about ten years later. In a 1971 *Washington Post* article, reporter William H. Jones wrote: "District Grocery Stores Inc., a cooperative venture of Washington merchants for nearly 52 years, has begun to liquidate its business—heralding the end of an era when so-called mom and pop stores dotted every neighborhood and thrived on the convenience offered nearby residents. Although DGS was able to survive the Great Depression and even to grow during the formative years of the great supermarket chains, it suffered immensely from the 1968 rioting in the city and finally was killed last summer when supermarkets began late night and Sunday hours."[40]

THE COLLECTIVE BUYING POWER that enabled DGS stores to offer competitive pricing was no match for the variety offered by supermarkets. Yet, Jones's article hints also at the fact that it was not purely market forces that hurt small grocers and the neighborhoods they served. The 1968 uprisings, the inequalities they represented, signified that food access was not simply a market problem; it was also a racism problem.

In D.C., people protested Martin Luther King's death and the racism that killed him for six days. Mourning and anger manifested in material losses, and the devastation of infrastructure was an impetus for future disinvestment and abandonment. Narrative accounts and newspaper articles suggest that businesses chose to relocate outside the District as a direct result of the riots, but out-migration of whites and Black middle-class families began before the riots, and so too did the out-migration of businesses. The riots, however, provide an example of how narratives of violence intertwined with Blackness become integral to justifying the systematic demise of access.

Deindustrialization and disinvestment in city centers, which accelerated in the 1970s, further contributed to the development of "black ghettoes" that were characterized by blight, poverty, unemployment, the influx of drugs, and increasing crime rates.[41] Using the term "racialized urban ghettos," Tony Whitehead suggests that it was not simply the blight, poverty, unemployment, or crime rates that characterized these neighborhoods. Their isolation from nonpoor areas—particularly the suburbs—was just as important, because access to limited and subpar resources contributed to continued decline.[42]

At the same time that Black neighborhoods were discursively and spatially ghettoized, many Black middle-class families left the city for nearby Prince George's County, Maryland, and beyond. As Sabiyha Prince notes, this migration was largely voluntary, as middle-class Blacks sought more space and increased safety.[43] It took place under different conditions than those that shaped the development of Black enclaves in the 1920s, 1930s, and 1940s. This voluntary migration highlighted class distinctions that, whether voluntarily or involuntarily, influenced the future development of predominantly African American neighborhoods, particularly those like Deanwood where entrepreneurship and shared racial identity created spaces where people of varying economic means lived in close proximity. For Deanwood, the physical and social isolation that caused it to be characterized as "the country" continued to be one of its greatest barriers to growth, especially as other neighborhoods developed and grew. A new paradigm related to race, space, and access developed.

The built environment in Washington, D.C., drastically changed post-1968, particularly in terms of grocery store access. By 1971, supermarkets reduced their stores by 24 percent. As William H. Jones noted in a 1971 article in the *Washington Post* cited earlier, supermarkets followed a national trend, choosing to leave predominantly Black inner-city neighborhoods in favor of more affluent, white suburban areas. By 1982, the number of major grocery stores had fallen to thirty-three, down from ninety-one in 1968 (see figures 2 and 3).[44]

Although Safeway initially maintained sixty-one stores in the District, forty-five of them in Black neighborhoods in 1971, that number dwindled to thirty-one by 1978. Between 1978 and 1981, Safeway reduced the number of stores in the District from thirty-one to twenty-five,[45] contradicting strong remarks the company's representatives made about the importance of maintaining grocery stores in inner cities to meet the basic needs of residents.[46] In 1980, the Safeway in Deanwood closed. A spokesperson remarked that the company closed the store because it had been "unprofitable for some time."[47]

Perhaps predictably, supermarkets followed wealthy and white people, many of whom left the city in favor of suburban areas. The number of employed D.C. residents declined from just under 320,000 in 1988 to about 280,000 in 1993.[48] Washington, D.C.'s population steadily declined from its peak of 800,000 in 1965 to 638,328 in 1980, and then to 572,059 in 2000.[49]

Food Chains Reduce Operations in D.C.

By William H. Jones
Washington Post Staff Writer

Big supermarket chains — with the single exception of Safeway Stores, Inc., the number two food retailer in the nation — are gradually reducing their stores in the predominantly black inner city of Washington.

Approximately 25 chain store units — many of them small by modern supermarket standards — have been closed in the city in recent years; fewer than 80 supermarket units survive. In addition, industry officials state that up to a dozen present locations might be closed or sold; none of the companies plan any new stores in the District, although Safeway is studying sites for possible expansion.

In the wake of this, a nucleus for a black-owned and operated supermarket chain has been formed — in some cases with the help of the chain retailers.

The first unit in the proposed chain of independently minority-owned grocery stores was formally dedicated yesterday at 1805 Columbia Rd., NW, as a "Big-V" supermarket. Until several weeks ago the store had been a unit of the Grand Union Co.

According to Allan Gallant, a supermarket specialist with the National Council for Equal Business Opportunity, the exodus from inner cities of supermarket chains is a nationwide development; the supermarkets are concentrating in relatively-affluent and relatively-white residential areas, he said.

The trend is not universal, however; in Chicago, the big Jewell Company chain—sixth largest food retailer in the U.S.—set up an affiliated company with ownership that now operates 19 stores in the inner city.

In Washington, Safeway has 61 stores in the city—45 of them in black neighborhoods. Ronald Zachary, spokesman for Safeway here, said yesterday that "one of the most serious problems this country is faced with is the exodus of businesses from high-density, low-income areas, especially with services as basic as food . . . we would urge other businesses to serve all the area's communities."

Great Atlantic & Pacific Tea Co., largest food retailer with U.S. sales of $5.8 billion (Oakland-based Safeway had sales last year of $4.8 billion), operates six A&P stores in the city and plans no new units, according to an official in A&P's regional office in Baltimore.

Acme Markets, 5th largest U.S. food retailer, used to operate a chain of small supermarkets in the District which were closed in the mid-1960's. Late in 1969, however, Acme promoted with banners and ribbon-cutting its "return" to Washington with a large store at 45 L St., SW.

At the time, Acme announced it would expand with future stores in the city; today the L Street store is closed and Acme has no expansion plans here—although its suburban and Baltimore area stores remain profitable.

Another one of the ten largest national food chains is the Grand Union Co., which is currently in the process of terminating all retail operations in the city. Washington-based Giant Food, Inc., has nine D.C. stores—mostly in relatively affluent areas of the city—and plans no new units here.

As for the new chains locating in the metropolitan area—such as Lucky Stores' Memco units and the S.S. Kresge K-Marts, which feature full discount supermarkets — no D.C. stores are planned.

Vincent P. Maguire, director of merchandising here for Grand Union, said his company's decision to shut down or sell all D.C. stores was based on the fact that the city stores were either unprofitable or, at best, marginally profitable.

Joseph B. Danzansky, Giant Food's president—and president of the Metropolitan Washington Board of Trade—said the costs of large enough plots of land for supermarkets made new units in D.C. "prohibitive" at this time.

Speaking at yesterday's Big-V grand opening, D.C. Del.-Elect Walter E. Fauntroy chided businesses for leaving the city while consumers have to remain behind. He asked citizens to support new businesses that are being formed "to fill the vacuum."

Safeway has agreed to help the new chain by providing free training for all Big-V employees; at the point where four Big-V units are operational, Safeway plans to provide management assistance in the person of an individual who will help in supervision. At least one Safeway unit that has been closed may reopen as a Big-V.

The other chains — such as Grand Union — are also helping to facilitate a change in ownership to black entrepreneurs.

FIGURE 2 Decline of grocery stores in D.C. documented by *The Washington Post and Times-Herald* as early as 1971. From *The Washington Post and Times-Herald*, 1 April 1971 © 1971.

The Grocery Stores' Flight To the Suburbs

By SANDRA R. GREGG

Washington Post Staff Writer

A new study commissioned by the city estimates that District food stores lose from $60 million to $120 million dollars a year to the suburbs. The study of Washington's food services, conducted by the University of the District of Columbia's Institute of District Affairs, also said that the number of major groceries here has shrunk from 91 in 1968 to 33 last year, and that the city needs as many as 20 more moderate-sized grocery stores.

Lawrence P. Shumake, director of the city's Office of Business and Economic Development, says the shortage of major supermarkets takes jobs and tax dollars away from the city.

"We can reverse that trend," Shumake insists. "There is public land that can be leveraged." OBED officials agree that there are a few abandoned lots and surplus federal land, such as Camp Simms in Southeast, that could be leased or sold to supermarket developers at a low price.

While many District residents polled in the study believed that small profits, shoplifting and crime are major factors that drive stores out of the city, store managers cited other reasons. Those who run the major chain groceries reported that they were less concerned about crime than they are about employe pilferage and what they said were shrinking profits from their smaller, less well-stocked stores.

Both store owners and city economists say the more important reason why supermarket chains are closing smaller stores in the District is because small stores are becoming outmoded and understocked, which company officials say keeps their profits low. The same officials say that because the city has little available land upon which these stores can expand or build new facilities with parking lots, they have to relocate to the suburbs or build bigger stores on the few large parcels of land they can get. Spokesmen for several major grocery store chains said that the trend now is toward larger stores that sell a variety of products including food, clothing and appliances.

"The larger stores emphasize one-stop shopping," said Giant spokeswoman Susan Portney. She also said that Giant is adding profitable sections such as pharmacies to its stores.

Closing these smaller stores can dent the morale of a community and often reduces the customer traffic to nearby shops. Because they attract customers, large department and grocery stores are often "anchors" around which smaller businesses like drug stores, shoe stores, dry cleaners and bakeries build.

The recent closing of a Safeway at 12th and Quincy streets NE in Brookland is an example of this problem. Safeway claimed the small store was not bringing in enough money. Its closing means shoppers will have less reason to come back to that area. Merchants along the 12th Street strip say the Safeway's closing already has begun to reduce business in their stores.

City officials say that finding space for large stores is difficult. The draft of the UDC study, prepared last week, said that all wards except Ward 3—west of Rock Creek Park—did not have enough food stores to meet the needs of local residents.

Jerome Paige, UDC professor of economics and

See STORES, Page 3, Col. 1

FIGURE 3 Grocery stores leave the District for suburban areas. From *The Washington Post*, 25 February 1982 © 1982.

The decline in population was not uniformly distributed. Wards 1, 2, and 3 experienced modest population gains between 1980 and 1990. Ward 1's population grew from 70,124 to 71,005, a 1.3 percent increase.[50] Ward 2's population grew from 56,986 to 59,457, a 4.3 percent change, and Ward 3's population grew from 68,919 to 74,271, a 7.8 percent change.[51] The populations in Wards 4, 5, 6, 7, and 8 each decreased. Ward 7, where Deanwood is located, had the sharpest change, losing 15.3 percent of its residents.[52] A 1994 headline in the *Washington Post* announced, "Declining Population Saps D.C.: As Residents Leave, Age, City's Tax Base Withers"; the article showed that D.C.

area suburbs such as Frederick County, Loudon County, and Calvert County experienced growth spurts while the city struggled to retain population.[53]

Washington, D.C., was not unique in the experience of supermarkets leaving cities to follow the money and white people to the suburbs. As food retailers continued to consolidate and monopolize the market, stores located in low-income and Black neighborhoods were steadily eliminated.[54] Publications from the *Washington Times*, to *Chain Store Age Executive*, to the *Wall Street Journal* published articles with headlines like "Elderly and Poor Are Victims of Flight of the Supermarkets," "Are Minorities Neglected? Riots Put New Slant on Old Question," and "Poor Selection: An Inner-City Shopper Seeking Healthy Food Finds Offerings Scant."[55]

In the midst of supermarkets closing stores in predominantly Black neighborhoods, executives from Safeway and Giant mentored Black entrepreneurs who wanted to open grocery stores (see figures 4 and 5). Super Pride, a Black-owned grocery chain, opened in 1981 in the building Safeway had previously occupied in Deanwood. Super Pride was part of Community Foods, a Baltimore-based chain of Black-owned grocery stores. At the time it opened its first and only store in D.C., Community Foods had operated in Baltimore for eleven years and maintained six stores. The chain's founder, Charles T. Burns, received part of his training in grocery store management from Safeway, the largest grocery chain in the country. Neither Burns nor the store manager had any known intimate ties to businesses or families in Deanwood. However, they specialized in serving inner-city communities and positioned Super Pride as an opportunity to provide both food and jobs in a neighborhood reeling from a mass exodus of middle-class residents.[56] Super Pride attempted to fill many—perhaps too many—gaps: a gap in food access, a gap in employment, and a gap in the economic sustainability in the neighborhood. Super Pride was not alone. George Shelton, who "defied skeptics who said a black-owned supermarket couldn't make it on Capitol Hill," opened a second store in 1980, predating Super Pride.[57] In 1982, Douglas Goggins open a 12,500-square-foot store in Buffalo, New York, under a unique name: FIGMOS-PTL (Finally I Got My Own Store—Praise The Lord). Goggins hoped to build consumers' confidence in Black-owned businesses and build community.[58] In Columbus, Ohio, Black residents were urged to support Singletary Plaza Mart, which was reportedly the largest Black-owned supermarket in the nation when it opened in 1984. Support did not necessarily materialize, as one column in the *Columbus Dispatch* outlined funding challenges for Singletary Plaza Mart under the headline "Hopes Outweigh Reality in PlazaMart Proposal."[59] In Richmond,

Black-owned Grocery Chain Brings Service Back to NE Neighborhood

By Brenda A. Russell
Washington Post Staff Writer

Residents of the Deanwood and Burrville communities in Northeast Washington last week formally welcomed a new black-owned, chain-operated supermarket in the store that had been occupied by Safeway until it closed last November.

For the area's nearly 20,000 residents, most of whom are elderly or without cars, the new 18,100-square-foot Super Pride at 51st Street and Nannie Helen Burroughs Avenue NE is eliminating the need for them to take a bus or taxi to the next nearest supermarket — a Safeway — located 10 blocks away.

Super Pride, which opened its doors two months ago, was officially welcomed by Mayor Marion Barry at special ceremonies arranged by the management.

"It means a lifesaver to me," declared Omie Cheeks, 60, who had grown accustomed to carrying her groceries from the old Safeway to her home at 5348 Nannie Helen Burroughs Ave., less than a block away. "Only time I've ever felt neglected was when they took the grocery store away."

Josephine Fuller of 814 52nd St. NE said she had to catch a bus to the Safeway at Minnesota and H streets NE. "I was one person who had to go a long way."

The neighborhood has several other stores. Across the avenue from the new market are a

See MARKET, Page 4, Col. 1

FIGURE 4   *The Washington Post* highlights Super Pride's arrival in Deanwood. From *The Washington Post*, 2 July 1981 © 1981.

Johnathan Johnson hoped that Community Pride Food Stores, Inc., which operated five stores in the city, would expand into predominantly Black neighborhoods that had been neglected by larger chains. Before the store opened in 1992, many residents traveled miles to buy groceries.[60] All these stores opened in predominantly Black neighborhoods that struggled with food security. All opened with a similar goal. Black entrepreneurs used market-based skills, attempting to fill a need for communities they presumably had a connection to, even if that connection was only racial identity.

This investment in Black neighborhoods was as much a reflection of the commitment of these businesses to self-reliance as it was about profit. Relying on building relationships with customers, offering sales on food items presumed to be important to Black foodways, and employing neighborhood residents, they positioned supermarkets to meet intersectional needs. While acknowledging that the government plays a critical role in the development of Black neighborhoods, in 1994, John Jacob, then president of the Urban League, stressed self-reliance: "Any group that waits for outside forces to come into the community and lift them up is doomed to be sitting there 20 years from now wishing and waiting."[61]

Both Safeway and Super Pride were invested in and reified the notion that Black-owned businesses were solutions and saviors in Black neighborhoods. However, integration, increased access to other parts of the city, brand

Come to Think of It, We Were Pretty Self-Sufficient   39

Soul Food and Price Specials Sustain Super Pride Success

By ISABEL WILKERSON

Special to The Washington Post

Whenever the Rev. Albert T. Davis gets his occasional, undeniable urge for fresh, plump porgies, he makes a half-hour trip from his upper Northwest home, bypassing several chain supermarkets, to the Super Pride store in far Northeast, where he figures he can get the best deal.

Operating out of a former Safeway store at 5110 Nannie Helen Burroughs Ave. NE, Super Pride is the District's largest black-owned and -operated supermarket and, with 40 workers, one of Ward 7's biggest employers.

The store not only caters to the specialized needs and tastes of its predominately black clientele in the Deanwood area, just west of the Maryland line, but in the process, draws customers from all over the metropolitan area with its merchandising formula.

"It's not that you can't get the kind of food that we sell at any other store," said general manager Edward Brown, referring to the chitterlings, hog's heads, pig's tails, and pork feet, brains and skins that line the Super Pride shelves. "It's just that we have more of what our people want and can keep the prices down. For the other stores, it's a guessing game as to how much to sell."

The demand for Super Pride's supply of "soul food" keeps the store's workers busy restocking display cases, particularly during holidays.

"Rather than one row of this or a couple of packages of that, we put up eight-foot spreads of black-eyed peas, collards and yams," Brown said. "We can hardly keep Jiffy cornbread mix on the shelves."

In an average week, Brown esti-

See STORE, Page 7, Col. 1

FIGURE 5 *The Washington Post* follows Super Pride's success, highlighting "soul food" as a primary factor. From *The Washington Post*, 12 January 1982 © 1983.

loyalty, and movement to the suburbs in part altered the meanings of Black neighborhoods and what it meant to support Black-owned businesses. Super Pride closed its doors in Deanwood, and its parent company closed three stores in Baltimore in June 2000.[62] Three months later, the company decided to close all its remaining stores. In an interview with the *Baltimore Business Journal*, Super Pride's president, Oscar A. Smith Jr., said that population decline was one of the reasons the store had not been able to stay open — "the same stores are fighting for fewer dollars."[63] Being a small, independent company, Super Pride could not absorb those losses, and while small companies like it were drowning, corporations like Giant and Safeway selectively maintained stores in parts of the city.

As residents watched food access decline, they also saw the ramifications of the influx of crack cocaine in their neighborhood. In the same *Baltimore Business Journal* article mentioned earlier, Oscar A. Smith Jr. alluded to drug sales in Black neighborhoods as being another factor that negatively impacted communities and food sales.[64] In Washington, D.C., Deanwood became a prime spot for open-air crack markets and other drug trading. In 1987, the

D.C. Commission of Public Health sponsored the second annual Drug Free D.C. Day in Deanwood at the corner of Division Avenue and Nannie Helen Burroughs Avenue. The location of the rally was strategic, in part to gain support from the community in the fight against drug abuse. Nestled against the Maryland state line, Deanwood was an ideal location for drug trafficking and sales. Albert Pickett, who was interviewed by a staff writer from the *Washington Post,* said that "his street [was] often lined with cars bearing suburban tags, as strangers stop[ped] in the neighborhood to purchase drugs."[65] The drug problem was much bigger than Deanwood, but the neighborhood was in the thick of it. What is now known as Marvin Gaye Park was a convenient location for selling and using, because thick trees shielded the area. When police patrolled the area, the grove provided ample time for someone to warn people to scatter.

The population in the Deanwood area decreased by 3,000 people between 1980 and 1990, the greatest change in thirty years.[66] For those who stayed, however, the effects of crack were seen not only in the population decline. They were seen in neighbors, family, and friends. Daron was a forty-year-old Deanwood native who moved back to the neighborhood after college. Daron's teenage years in the 1980s and 1990s were caught between a history of self-reliance through which he himself had not lived and an influx of crack, the effects of which he saw in the lives of his neighbors:

Once the recreation center was closed, the jobs left, crack poured into our community. This was the odd part; we knew systematically that it was not by our doing. We were really well educated on our history, the civil rights movement, art, music, culture, business; we understood the implications that this created. The morality of the people was waning, because the first people that it hit were our parents. The generation right above me started abusing. I'm 40, so I would say the 45 to 55 generation . . . LSD, PCP, crack. We didn't have a real good example . . . What I saw happen was, the generation that was raised in my generation, disappeared . . . dealing drugs. They locked up all the men first. The women were left to fend for themselves. You had grandparents raising babies. It was the beginning of the end. We saw it as such. I watched about 40 guys that played ball with me . . . I'd say about 13 of us, 12 of us now, only six or seven of us made it out without criminal records. I mean that literally. I'm not exaggerating. A lot of us went to college, despite the fact that we got in trouble. Most of us got caught up in the law system.

Daron's narrative offers connections between structural changes and the effects of crack on Deanwood residents. Yet, his narrative also highlights the limits of self-reliance as an antidote to systemic failures. Shifts in residents' consciousness and practices accompanied the sociopolitical changes in population and grocery store access. Participants grappled with these changes; they questioned and critiqued the changes in food production and consumption practices and community cohesion.

While supermarkets' importance increased, gardening and subsistence farming decreased. Increasing access to public transportation, other neighborhoods that were perceived to be better than Deanwood, the quickening pace of American life, and a burgeoning food revolution centering supermarkets influenced food production. Deanwood residents integrated themselves into these changes. Changing notions of progress and modernity complicated the concept of self-reliance upon which Deanwood was founded. This was a seminal shift in Deanwood's history, one that served as a cornerstone for participants in my study as they grappled with the relationships between community cohesion and low food access.

Conclusion

Deanwood's history suggests that even in the face of inequities, residents have consistently exhibited agency in their community building, food production, and consumption. Education, homeownership, and entrepreneurship were key components of resisting racism through self-reliance. Though they experienced racial exclusion elsewhere, early Deanwood residents invested their money, time, and talents in developing a community in which they felt safe and nourished by both the businesses and the social relationships. Thus, the first half of the twentieth century produced a Black enclave that had "the material and symbolic expression of success."[67]

The industrialization of food production and distribution in the United States altered the national foodscape and Deanwood's local foodscape. Local food producers and sellers—like hucksters, the mothers who sold their food products from home, and the small grocers on nearly every street—were casualties in a shift toward the convenience of larger, better-stocked stores. As the nation's food system became more industrialized and usurped by the market economy, residents became more dependent on supermarkets, unknowingly contributing to the destabilization of Deanwood's local foodscape. Without the local food practices upon which Deanwood's food security was partially based, the neighborhood's food access was at the mercy of the increasingly transnational food corporations that systematically left Black neighborhoods in favor of the suburbs. All these changes in food access were embedded in, not separate from, national trends in racial segregation and inequalities that shaped access to resources and opportunities. Within this context, Black entrepreneurship in the form of small stores in the first half of the twentieth century, as well as supermarket chains like Super Pride in the 1980s, reflected how important entrepreneurship was to addressing food inequalities that Black residents did not create.

This was the context my research participants navigated during my fieldwork. They not only negotiated where to shop; they also grappled with framing, understanding, and reconciling Deanwood's food access in social, economic, and ideological contexts. This included deciding where to grocery shop, using gardening as a form of resistance, and positioning Community Market as a symbol of a past Deanwood that no longer exists. I examine each of these in subsequent chapters, demonstrating multiple strategies used to navigate food access in and beyond the neighborhood.

CHAPTER TWO

There Ain't Nothing in Deanwood
Navigating Nothingness and the UnSafeway

> Because I am a family of five, I have to go frequent to the
> grocery store quite often. And a lot of times I have to go over to the
> Maryland side, because of the quality of food at the Safeway on
> Minnesota Avenue. Or there is not a grocery store in a good maybe
> five-mile, maybe more, vicinity.
>
> —RESEARCH PARTICIPANT

> They have a nickname for the Safeway. We call it the unSafeway.
>
> —RESEARCH PARTICIPANT

Caylon was a biracial, formerly incarcerated twenty-six-year-old single
father. On the day of our interview, I met him at his job at a local nonprofit
that served homeless and underemployed D.C. residents. The food pantry
was open that day, and people crowded the hallways, waiting to receive a
ration of the organization's supply. Caylon led the way through the crowd
toward a back room. It was less of an office and more of a community room
that could be sectioned into smaller spaces by room dividers. Caylon pulled
out a chair for me, told his colleague that he was going to be doing an interview, and pulled the divider closed to give us a little privacy. I could still hear
the small group of people meeting on the other side as Caylon sat across from
me. I invited Caylon to start wherever he'd like, assuring him that I was con-
fident we would eventually get around to everything I wanted to touch on
during the interview. Caylon began:

> *There ain't nothing in Deanwood.* There's no grocery stores. From
> Chevron [gas station] to the Maryland [state] line, coming from the
> Maryland line, you have, on the DC side, the 7-11, the carryout across
> the street, the liquor store, and the old car wash. If you come down—
> down Chevron. Come at, I mean, going back into the DC way, and you
> get down by Jay Street and 47th Place, there's nothing but Brown's
> Liquor, across the street is another corner store, there's a cleaners and
> if you [go] down a little more there's another corner store and there's
> nothing to eat right down that whole strip and then well, you have to

go all the way around the corner, which is nothing but McDonald's and Wendy's. That's it and Mickey's and Suburb Liquor. That's it. *There ain't nothing in Deanwood.* [emphasis added]

Nothingness consistently factored into residents' responses concerning how, where, and how often they accessed the groceries they needed to feed themselves and their families. Caylon, like the majority of people in cities, primarily relied on grocery stores to meet his family's food needs. Supermarkets, modeling a trend in convenience in American consumerism, ideally make grocery shopping easier. For Black urban residents, however, they become another manifestation of inequities that shape access to a number of resources.

As explored in chapter 1, the food inequities that residents navigated did not appear overnight. White and middle-class flight, changing consumer culture, and the growth of supermarkets—all touched by anti-Black racism in one way or another—influenced the structure of neighborhood, local, national, and global food systems.[1] American exceptionalism and a meritocracy that favors those who are already privileged create conditions under which accessing food, and the barriers to accessing food, can be viewed as individual concerns—not systemic ones. However, contemporary cities across the United States reflect the effects of racial segregation on the food system. When supermarket access is mapped according to the racial composition of neighborhoods, it shows that predominantly Black neighborhoods have less access than their white counterparts.[2] On a day-to-day basis, these macro-level inequities in the food system create everyday challenges for those navigating the local food system.

Nothingness—empty, void—is a consistent theme in food access literature and, as Caylon's words suggest, a refrain that is not uncommon for residents themselves to adopt. Early research served to highlight disparities, particularly to demonstrate how disparities in grocery store access resulted in poor and urban dwellers paying more for food.[3] This scholarship provided a critical intervention in studies of both urban spaces and urban health, as it laid a foundation for thinking about the ways in which structural inequities are barriers to eating well and living a healthy life. David Williams and Chiquita Collins's assertion that racial residential segregation is a fundamental cause of health disparities, and Elizabeth Eisenhauer's articulation that supermarket redlining followed patterns of residential segregation, monumentally shifted conversations, and in the past fifteen years, scholarship on race and the food system has become a standard in food studies.[4]

There have been shortcomings and consequences of the deficit model outlined by scholars. As scholarly and public attention shifted more toward access inequities, researchers, policymakers, and community-based organizations and activists turned to terms like "food desert," a shorthand for inequities that overemphasizes lack and very rarely examines agency or resilience among community members. Further, the term, which some academics and activists have argued is inaccurate and racist, often obscures the processes that led to unequal access and reflects a long-standing interest in uncritical and negative evaluations of Black communities and people.[5] The assumption of lack becomes inscribed in their bodies, evident in the ways nonprofits, advocates, researchers, and policymakers frame residents' lack of knowledge or will to access or eat healthier foods, rather than locating the deficiencies in the ways white supremacy has shaped neighborhood food spaces.[6] So while acknowledging disparities, recent scholarship has often re-inscribed the narratives of nothingness that pervade the national conversation concerning Black people and accessing food at the expense of examining the fullness of Black lives at the intersection of inequities. What happens when we examine lack, choice, and decision making as dynamic and inter-related processes in accessing food?

Some have critiqued the supply-side approach that characterizes many conversations about lack and are clear that focusing on supermarkets as an explanation of this inequality at the exclusion of other components of food-ways is insufficient.[7] As the alternative food and food justice movements gain momentum, urban farming and agriculture take center stage as central to reimagining a broken food system. The reality remains, however, that the majority of consumers continue to rely heavily on grocery stores, even if they incorporate gardening, urban farming, or farmers' markets in their food consumption. The Food Marketing Institute (FMI) reported that there were 38,441 supermarkets in the United States in 2016.[8] Further, the whiteness of the alternative food movement and the relatively limited reach of Black-led food justice efforts mean that the majority of urban residents are disconnected from these alternatives, even if they are available in their neighborhoods. For most, urban agriculture has yet to figure prominently into their daily lives, and the supermarket remains central to current food procurement practices. While the absence of grocery stores is a vital component of understanding urban food inequities, to begin and end a conversation with their physical geography ignores the multifaceted ways residents understand, critique, and navigate their absence. The question, then, is *How do residents navigate nothingness when grocery stores are the pre-eminent component of acquiring food in the contemporary food system?*

This chapter presumes that supermarkets continue to be important sites for analysis, particularly in terms of understanding how residents themselves understand their function, critique them, and devise ways to navigate them when they are absent or do not meet their needs or preferences. The chapter begins where chapter 1 ended, exploring the contemporary unequal food system in Washington, D.C. Then it shifts to examine the shopping experiences of Deanwood's economically diverse residents, taking into account agency and preferences in the context of residents' decision making regarding where to shop.

Washington, D.C.: An Unequal Food Landscape

In Washington, D.C., as in many other cities in the United States, the chance of a full-service grocery store being nearby depends on where a person lives. And, as research has shown, where a person lives is highly dependent on race and class.[9] Politically and geographically organized into smaller units known as wards, Washington, D.C., reflects race and class inequities that plague other U.S. cities — one of the legacies of enduring racial segregation. The Anacostia River has long been a dividing line for both spatial inequities that reflect unequal access to resources and embodied, lived experiences patterned along race and class divisions. Harry Jaffe and Tom Sherwood illustrate the paradox of communities east of the Anacostia River being simultaneously connected and disconnected: "Five bridges cross the Anacostia, but the people who live there are disconnected and easy to abandon. Not all are poor, but nearly 100 percent are African-American, and too many are dispossessed."[10] Deanwood is located in Ward 7, which — along with Ward 8 — is located east of the Anacostia River. Collectively, Wards 7 and 8 — both overwhelmingly Black — are ecologically isolated and disadvantaged compared to the city's other wards. Both represent the lowest average household income and the highest percentages of overweight or obese residents and those with diabetes. Unsurprisingly, when grocery store access is mapped in D.C., residents of communities east of the Anacostia shoulder the heaviest burden (see maps 2 and 3).

In 2010, Ward 7 had four full-service grocery stores. By 2017, that number had declined to two. Ward 8's full-service grocery stores dwindled from three to one in the same time frame.[11] Collectively, these three supermarkets

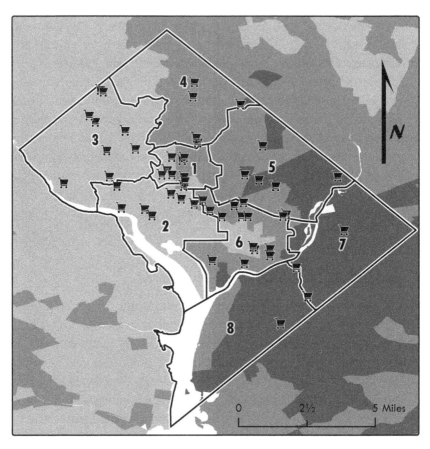

Grocery Store Locations

Percent Population Black or African American Alone*

Less than 20%
Between 20–80%
Greater than 80%

*ACS 2016 5-year estimates

MAP 2 Grocery store locations and percentage Black or African American population. Map courtesy of Emeline Renz (@mapgrrl).

serve nearly 150,000 residents east of the Anacostia River. The stores are overcrowded and understocked, two of the most voiced complaints about the supermarket closest to Deanwood, a Safeway that many avoid altogether when possible. In an attempt to prevent thefts and perhaps protect customers, security guards flank each entrance of the Safeway nearest Deanwood, creating a surveilled food environment that mirrors the anti-Black policing that often occurs in predominantly Black neighborhoods. On average,

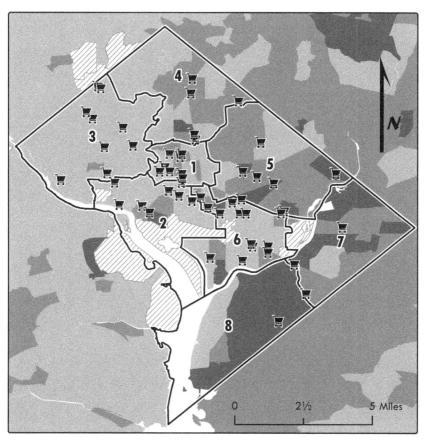

≤$37,753.00
≤$75,506.00**
≤$248,000.00
Undetermined

*ACS 2015 5-year estimates
**DC Median Household Income, Data.gov

MAP 3 Grocery store locations and median income. Map courtesy of
Emeline Renz (@mapgrrl).

wealthier, whiter wards not only have more grocery stores than predominantly African American wards, but also are more likely to have plans for
future stores. This has had implications for where people shop, frequenting
stores outside their neighborhood and, in many cases, outside the District,
which has reinforced the racialized and classed texture of accessing food (see
table 1).

TABLE 1 Changes in the number of confirmed and planned full-service grocery stores in Washington, D.C., from 2010 to 2016, compared to D.C.'s 2014 median household incomes and racial and ethnic demographics

Wards	# of Full-Service Grocery Stores, 2010	# of Full-Service Grocery Stores, 2016	# of Full-Service Grocery Stores in Pipeline, 2016	Median Household Income, 2014	% Non-Hispanic Black, 2014	% Non-Hispanic White, 2014	% Hispanic, Any Race, 2014
Ward 1	6	8	1	$80,794	31.4	54.7	20.8
Ward 2	8	7	0	$99,422	9.0	74.7	9.8
Ward 3	11	9	0	$109,909	6.0	82.2	9.4
Ward 4	2	5	1	$71,545	58.6	26.1	19.3
Ward 5	3	7	1	$55,063	72.8	18.3	8.3
Ward 6	4	10	3	$90,903	36.7	54.1	6.0
Ward 7	4	2	0	$39,828	94.4	2.5	2.8
Ward 8	3	1	0	$31,642	93.7	4.3	1.4
D.C. Overall	41 (avg. 5.1 per ward)	49 (avg. 6.1 per ward)	6 (avg. 0.75 per ward)	$69,235	49.6	40.2	9.9

Source: The data presented in this table comes from the "Closing the Grocery Store Gap in the Nation's Capital" report, published by D.C. Hunger, a nonprofit organization in Washington, D.C., committed to eradicating food insecurity in 2016.

The Anacostia River, then, is a figurative and literal reminder of the city's segregation, the context in which residents physically, socially, and ideologically navigate the daily reminders of the multiple ways anti-Black racism has shaped the contours of their spatial contexts, including accessing food. Not all the participants in my study were "poor folks" or in the most precarious economic or social conditions, as Jaffe and Sherwood pointed out, but the neighborhood in which they lived, though rich with history and landownership, reflected what sociologists have discovered: that even when inhabited by middle-class families, predominantly Black neighborhoods, on average, have fewer resources than predominantly white neighborhoods.[12]

What residents demonstrated is that the unequal spatial geography of grocery stores in the District reflected systematic failures in the food system but that those failures did not necessarily translate to lack in their lives. Even, for example, as participants pointed out what was missing—highlighting nothingness, as Caylon did—they also demonstrated the opposite of lack: strategizing, informed decision making, and nuanced understandings of not only the systematic failures of the food system but also what they desired in a shopping experience. Understanding the geographic distribution of grocery stores reveals spatial inequities. Understanding how people navigated this geographic distribution reveals what residents do when faced with those spatial inequities. If the goal is to increase accessibility, then it is not enough to know where a new grocery store can be added. Individuals' and communities' desires for their own foodways are critical components for creating sustainable, equitable interventions.

(*Un*)Safeway

"Do you think you offer quality food and service here in your store?" a news reporter asked the store manager as they stood in front of a meat display. In August 2017, the Safeway in Ward 7, one of its two supermarkets, was under scrutiny after moldy produce and expired meat were discovered by Ward 7's councilperson during a surprise visit. "I think we do," he replied. "We've had where people come and open up packages and we'll come back and look and say 'oh somebody has opened this up.' We've found meat in other departments. A few weeks ago, someone was shot in the area. So, then, just like I told the young lady, sometimes we have people come in, you know, who are great . . ." The reporter interrupted him with the question, "Do you think this is a more challenging area to run a grocery store?" The manager was prompt with his response: "No. No, that's not what I'm saying. What I'm saying is we want to make sure that the well-being of the customers and the well-being of the employees is taken care of."

Responses to the news report were almost uniform. People who shopped at the Safeway took to social media, listservs, and one-on-one conversations to lament its lack of quality food and quality service. A month later, a coalition of food justice organizations in D.C. organized a grocery walk to bring attention to the lack of access to fresh, affordable, and healthy food east of the Anacostia River. Beginning at the only supermarket in Ward 8, participants walked two miles, approximately forty-five minutes, to central Anacostia, a predominantly Black neighborhood that has become emblematic of city and national policies that upend Black communities and of increasing gentrification in the city. The news report and the subsequent grocery walk increased public attention to what residents in my study indicated in their survey responses and interviews: that the Safeway that served their neighborhood had several problems and was among the least desirable places to shop for groceries, and that they deserved not only more stores but higher quality.

In the 2016 survey I conducted with a collaborator from the neighborhood, respondents were more likely to be on the upper end of the income spectrum, higher than the median income for Deanwood specifically and Ward 7 more generally, and demonstrated that though the area was designated as "low-income," Ward 7's economic diversity and rates of homeownership could not be ignored.[13] Among the eighty-seven respondents who completed the full survey, fifty-six reported incomes at or above $70,000 a year, were more likely to report owning their homes, and were less likely to shop for food within the neighborhood (see table 2).

The survey revealed that, even when not asked specifically, residents were ready and willing to share critiques of the local store. In the survey, residents were not asked about the Safeway specifically but were given an opportunity to provide open-ended, qualitative responses to indicate their shopping experiences at any of the stores they frequented in the city. Table 3 illustrates the range of responses about the nearby Safeway. Their responses reflected a variety of concerns, ranging from overcrowding to poor customer service and poor quality. Responses indicated that even when the Safeway was close or convenient, it was often not chosen as the first place to grocery shop for many residents, particularly those with transportation and more money (see table 3).

In ethnographic exploration with Deanwood residents, the responses were similar. Irma, a woman in her mid-sixties, had been a resident of Dean-

TABLE 2 Survey participants' demographics by self-reported income

	Total %	< $40,000 n=12	$40,000– $69,999 n=19	$70,000– $99,999 n=30	≥$100,000 n=26
Age in years (%)[1]					
18 to 34	31.4	16.7	36.8	33.3	26.9
35 to 44	28.1	16.7	26.3	30.0	34.6
45 to 54	20.8	8.3	26.3	23.3	23.1
55 to 64	14.8	25.0	10.5	13.3	7.7
65 or older	3.1	16.7	0.0	0.0	3.9
Female (%)	78.1	66.7	79.0	80.0	76.9
Marital status (%)					
Currently married	33.7	16.7	21.1	25.0	57.7
Formerly married	22.8	50.0	31.6	17.86	11.5
Never married	43.5	33.3	47.4	57.1	30.8
Employment status (%)					
Working	82.8	33.3	94.7	86.7	88.5
Self-employed	7.5	16.7	0.0	13.3	3.9
Looking for work/ unable/retired/student	9.7	50.0	5.3	0.0	7.7
Neighborhood tenure in years (%)					
Less than 1 year	7.3	8.3	0.0	6.7	11.5
1 to 5 years	44.8	33.3	47.37	50.0	50.0
5 to 10 years	18.8	25.0	31.6	13.3	3.9
10 years or more	29.2	33.3	21.1	30.0	34.6
Homeowner (%)	84.0	58.3	77.8	86.7	92.3

1. Two people (about 2% of the sample) selected "I prefer not to say" in response to the question asking their age.

wood for nearly forty years. Like many of those who participated in the survey, she avoided the neighborhood Safeway as much as possible:

> The nearest thing we have is a Safeway, which is like, one of the worst places in the world. Okay? It's poorly managed. The prices are higher 'cause they have so much shrinkages they say. Then you know, you go to some stores, you going in and a bottle of soda is supposed to come up here [*makes reference to a full bottle with her hand*] and your soda is only coming up here [*makes reference to a less full bottle with her hand*],

TABLE 3 Ward 7 residents' open-ended responses about the local Safeway

The few times I've frequented the Safeway, the quality of options is poor[er]/[more] inferior than the stores I frequent in Virginia. In addition, quantities are limited and rarely do they have the items that are on sale. I really hate that I have to shop outside my community, but I don't have a choice.

I appreciate quality customer service and quality food. Most of the venues I listed [Yes Organic Market, Trader Joes, Whole Foods, Eastern Market, and Safeway] have both, with the exception of Safeway, where you have employees with a lack of knowledge on items they sell, typically, and overall neutral or negative attitudes towards customers.

Within [my neighborhood] the grocery experience is horrible. Regardless of what time you decide to shop at the local store, there are ALWAYS long lines, the prices seem higher, and I always feel watched. Regular items are not always in stock (example: cucumbers and Frosted Flakes cereal. I can't believe they didn't have the items).

The Safeway in Ward 7 is our supermarket of last resort. It's not bad but its produce and meat/dairy selections leave something to be desired, and we prefer both the price value and quality of Wegman's generic brands to Safeway's in most cases.

I try not to use the Safeway that's less than a half mile from my house. Family members and I have bought expired milk, soda, juice, and other items that may have been eaten by seniors or young children. Lines are usually long. Store is usually dirty and shelves are lean unless I go on Wednesday.

The Safeway near me isn't a terrible store, but it is often understaffed, with very long, slow lines. There are no self-checkout lines so there aren't really any quick options. I try to go there early in the morning on the weekends in order to avoid the lines.

I would love the opportunity to shop in my neighborhood, but the closest store is awful. Not only is it unclean and lacking fresh produce and fresh meat, people follow you around trying to get you to sign up for free phones and other non-grocery store items (all scams).

I usually travel more than ten minutes away from my home (outside of Ward 7) because the grocery stores near my home are usually crowded, with not enough cashiers, and are not well stocked. There are also frequent altercations in the parking lots of the stores near my home, and I bring my one-year-old with me shopping.

The Safeway is very close to my home. And while I love that aspect, the loitering and lack of basic needs such as baskets is a deterrent at times. Also, the long lines and lack of self-checkout when I only need one to three items.

The Safeway is dirty and doesn't have good-quality food.

Sadly, I have to leave the neighborhood for groceries. Do not like the Safeway that is within walking distance.

I really wish that retailers would stop this nonsense and build quality retail in Ward 7. The Safeway on Minnesota Avenue is a dump and needs to be burned down. The quality of food it sells to Ward 7 residents is sickening.

I have noticed that certain neighborhoods have better-quality items or quantity. I have to drive to Maryland because I live on the D.C. line. The only close grocery store is the Safeway. That store either has [a] limited amount of things, low staff which causes long lines, [or is] congested with panhandlers.

Safeway—worst shopping experience and very stressful. It is within easy walking distance.

Safeway is less than a minute drive from my house, but the selection is terrible. It is full of frozen food and junk. The organic produce is literally all put on one display and it's often empty and has old produce.

Safeway: very long lines, shopping carts are few and often don't work, very little help. Healthy options often not available (e.g., quinoa and almond milk are hard to find).

those kinds of things. Products sit on the shelf too long so it's not quality. You know, it's the last resort kind of place for me. I go to Maryland. I go to Shoppers Food Warehouse. I go to Wegman's. I go to Costco. Now we have a Costco in D.C.

Her neighbor, Anne, grew up in Deanwood. Her experiences with shopping for food varied over the course of her life, and included watching the life and death of a Safeway within the neighborhood's boundaries and of Super Pride, a Black-owned chain that opened in the 1980s and closed within the decade. For Anne, the primary concern with the Safeway was that it did not provide what she needed: "The food tends to, in this area, even the Safeway, it's basic. It's very basic, and I will only go there if I'm really early, early in the morning and I'm really in need of something or on a Sunday morning." Someone who sought out what she framed as "alternative" healthy products, Anne used the Safeway as a last resort. Instead, she traveled fifteen to twenty minutes to Wegman's in Prince George's County, Maryland, which offered not only what she wanted in terms of food but also a better shopping experience:

> I just thought Wegman's is wonderful, and those of us who can get over there. I mean, they just give a wide range of everything that you really want. I think of all the places that are nearby, that's probably the best. And they don't—It's interesting. You don't have people's children throwing tizzies. I'm good with eating cookies out of the box you know, doing real dramatic things. They really don't. I don't know how they do it. Once people walk in there, it's a whole different thing. That's probably because the majority of people that are in there override that kind of [*pause*] whatever.

Because of the resources they had their disposal, both Irma and Anne could avoid the local Safeway and "that kind of whatever" that Anne identified in her interview. Their access to resources is not tangential to their responses to and about the local Safeway. Instead, economic stability and having access to cars meant that it was easier for them to make different choices. Though Anne does not explicitly indicate what "that kind of whatever" is in her interview, her reference to children having temper tantrums acts as a foil to the unnamed and undescribed shoppers at Wegman's who presumably create a more palatable shopping experience for her. This, coupled with Irma's description of low quality, suggests that residents' understanding of quality included both spatial components and shopper characteristics.

If Anne's "that kind of whatever" was coded language to describe behaviors that led to unpleasant shopping experiences, Dametria's description of other shoppers was much more explicit:

> There [are] too many people coming in there that don't care about things. They see something, they get it, then they don't put it back. They leave it there. It's just too much, then you don't know if they're putting it back and it's going bad. It's too much. They're not taking care of the store. They don't care. They want more, but they don't take care of it. How can you get more when you don't take care of something? You want more? You need to take the initiative of taking care of your store.

Dametria's response echoes some of the sentiments of the store manager in the news segment mentioned earlier and reflects the types of contradictions born out of anti-Blackness and consistent unequal access to resources. Residents critique the store and recognize that access to food in D.C. is patterned along the lines of racial and economic segregation in the city. At the same time, some, as evidenced in Dametria's response, also critiqued store patrons. Both the store manager and Dametria turn to personal responsibility to partially explain the Safeway's subpar offerings, shifting some of the blame for the store's lack to the customers themselves. Dametria's response goes further to ask rhetorical questions concerning the worthiness of those who desire a better store. This dialectic—recognizing structural inequities while also placing blame or responsibility on those who are most affected by them—reflects deeply held beliefs that personal responsibility is paramount to accessing and maintaining high-quality resources, even in the face of corporate failures. Dametria's and others' concerns were layered, toggling between spatial and behavioral critiques.

Some of this reflects the same ethos that is foundational to self-reliance as an embodied theory of community uplift: that even when held accountable, the state and corporations will fail to meet the needs of Black people; and if those needs are to be met, a racialized asceticism, one in which every behavior counts (and the negative ones count double), is required. This is not to say self-reliance has not been a beneficial way of understanding what it means to operate within a nation-state that is fundamentally unequal. Neither does it mean that Dametria's comments can wholly be understood through a lens of neoliberal logic of individual responsibility filtering into the everyday lives of those in Deanwood. However, as Keeanga-Yamahtta Taylor argues, "American exceptionalism operates as a mythology of convenience that does a tremendous amount of work to simplify the contradiction between the apparent creed of US society and its much more complicated reality. Where people have failed to succeed and cash in on the abundance that American ingenuity has apparently created, their personal failures or deficiencies serve as an explanation."[14] This is no different for the food system. While there is evidence that Safeway does not meet high standards for its customers east of the Anacostia River, the deficiencies and failures of the corporation became embodied, fused with those interpreted to be personal ones. Here, lack or nothingness functions at the individual level. For Dametria, at least part of the lack or deficiency is located in the actions of those who shop at Safeway, reflecting a broader trend that looks to defects in Black people and culture despite the materiality produced by inequality.[15]

Between a Corner Store and a Safeway

It is not simply that people disliked the store. Given the uneven distribution of grocery stores and supermarkets in Washington, D.C., Safeway's quality mattered precisely because it was the closest. To seek out other stores meant that residents created food geographies outside their neighborhoods, which presented challenges for those who did not own cars or for whom the added time and money needed to travel outside the neighborhood were more significant than the awful shopping experience at Safeway. Kim, who lived alone in public housing, described nothingness in a different way, making a distinction between those who can get the food they want to eat and those who cannot. While she echoes concerns about quality and variety, similar to those voiced by Irma and Anne, Kim's socioeconomic status compounded precarity:

> Those shelves, one time they scared me. I didn't know . . . one time I said, "Let me check the noodles to see if there's a food shortage," because the whole place would be wiped out. The Safeway, if I go down there and they don't have what I need, I'm going to be ticked off already [*laughter*], you know because that has happened. So then you start looking, so you start with things like this: you found your favorite foods. I'm sure other businesses [have them] too, but where are they and is it worth going after, to sacrifice. So um, that's the difference between [us] and those who take food for granted and get everything they want to buy. And then you might want to say, "well how does that

affect consciousness?" Well, this: anything you have to stress about will take a little bit out of your day.

Kim's narrative is an example of one of the ways poor participants experienced and navigated the neighborhood food landscape in ways that embodied their class positions. Pointedly, she explained how distinction works: those with economic privilege take for granted the real ways she weighed sacrifice on a daily basis. With the exception of Anne, who acknowledged the privilege of having her own transportation, participants with more economic capital did not reflect on their privileges in their interviews. Whereas "essentials" such as time, money, and transportation figured prominently in interviews with participants who had less economic capital, these very same essentials were taken for granted in the interviews with their neighbors. Their interviews were more likely to emphasize the right to a quality shopping experience and store than stressors.

Mr. Harris, who did not own a car, indicated that one of the stressors he considered regularly was how to get to the grocery store. In his interview, he indicated that he would go wherever his friend liked to go, which influenced and constrained his choices in terms of where he would shop, because he depended on his friend for a ride. Even though he admitted that not having a car added extra stress to his daily life, Mr. Harris viewed this through a somewhat hopeful lens of what relying on neighbors meant for relationships, particularly for people like him who lived in public housing:

> Yeah. But um, yeah that's, that's the challenge is, is getting food back and forth and it's part of your day's *work*. When I was working and driving, it was entirely different. Most of us [living here] are depending on our own for food. We have neighbors that we can ride with . . . and here is what it does. It forces us to all to get and be neighborly. I mean, I don't care how bad the neighborhood is and it looks that terrible, you're going to find some people that have each other's back and that's what you have to go with. What happens is when you're in housing, public housing, people move and you miss them and there's nothing you can do about it. [emphasis added]

While there is debate about how or if having a supermarket nearby improves health, Mr. Harris's characterization of grocery shopping as work and Kim's notion of sacrifice suggest that qualitatively, stores matter more than measured health outcomes. They also factor into how residents think about their time, their lives, and what is considered work.

Mr. Harris's response also reflected his optimism about his neighbors and the community. He openly acknowledged the high crime rates, low literacy, and lack of involvement from some of his neighbors. However, Mr. Harris's commitment to the community garden (explored in depth in chapter 5), as well as the social and cultural development of his neighbors, was foundational to how he framed his neighbors and grocery shopping. Rather than painting a picture of residents as irresponsible consumers, he connected grocery shopping to being neighborly and to community cohesiveness. While he implicitly acknowledges that there is "bad" in the neighborhood, he also recognized that people have each other's backs, demonstrating forms of care that are often obscured in explorations of how life unfolds within public housing. This, compared to the ways policy and practice attempt to erase poor people's desires and choices, presents a radically different view of how residents in neighborhoods with unequal access navigate the food landscape around them.

Mr. Harris and others with no cars and limited income might have felt more compelled to discuss the role of their social networks in grocery shopping than their counterparts because it is ingrained in their day-to-day life, as Mr. Harris suggested. It required building relationships with neighbors and friends on whom they could rely. Vicky Cattell suggests that while features associated with neighborhoods play a role in how social networks form, the direct effects of such networks differ according to structural and cultural characteristics.[16] Thus, although my participants all lived in the same neighborhood, their social networks looked different, and the uses of those networks yielded different outcomes. In the case of residents who did not have their own transportation, this manifested in using those networks to get to the grocery store, for which the person who drove would get compensated in some way. When he did not ride with a friend, Mr. Harris rode his bike to the store, which meant negotiating which store to go to:

I have to go all the way down to the Safeway. This is . . . This is . . . it's good you're asking. Just take today. Today I really didn't want to pay my little 99 cents for my oven breads that I like from Safeway . . . I've been a little lazy. I didn't feel like going down there [laughs] for a walk, and I decided to go to the corner store. I paid double . . . that makes a difference in the choice of store. And it made a difference of about a half a mile. If I would have taken my bike, which I like to bike, I would have gone to the Safeway, but then I have to think, "is my bike gonna be outside when I get back?" because I don't have a lock. With the corner store, I can watch the bike . . . see these are real, really issues that now we think about on a daily basis.

Mr. Harris's narrative illustrates the intersection of several issues that shape the process of procuring food: cost, distance, desire, and safety. Mr. Harris does not own a car. His primary source of transportation—besides walking—is his bicycle. At the time of the interview, Mr. Harris was jobless and had limited income. He weighed the opportunity cost of shopping at Safeway as compared to the risk of his bike being stolen. In this way, Mr. Harris challenged the idea of absolute cost. Solely considering the price of foods, Safeway may have been cheaper, but adding in his bike as an additional factor reduced the lure of Safeway. Instead, he relied on the local corner store in between big grocery shopping trips.

Alison Alkon et al. demonstrate that food considerations of the urban poor are complex and are often restricted because of income rather than geography.[17] Yet, the residents in this study were clear that geography was a barrier, particularly when it came to making decisions about which stores and forms of transportation to choose. These barriers caused additional stress, on top of the already stress-inducing conditions produced by racism and income inequality.

Naa Oyo Kwate argues that time itself is a social determinant of health that perpetuates disparities for Black people. Meeting basic needs and the limited time allowed for meeting those needs manifest in stress and loss of quality years of life.[18] When applied to navigating the unequal food system, time spent traveling to grocery stores and even the stress induced by making a decision based on limited economic means or transportation are clearly concerns tied to the distribution of stores that residents primarily frequent. Kwate's argument reflects research that demonstrates that stress and race-based trauma contribute to health disparities and should be considered when assessing the quality of life of people of color in the United States.[19] In this way, traveling further or resigning oneself to purchasing inferior products—especially for the poor—is not merely about preferences, even when one can meet them. It is also a matter of life and death.

Pursuing Healthiness

For participants who were parents, their children were motivators in defining and pursuing healthy foods, even if they had economic or transportation constraints. Janice and Koti, for example, used Zipcar to travel to Virginia to purchase healthy, affordable food for their two children. Similar to Janice and Koti, Caylon, Dametria, and Mr. Harris factored their children into their consumption practices, though each rooted their concerns for healthiness in different frameworks. Caylon, for example, spoke at length about the restrictions his father placed on what he could eat during his childhood:

> CAYLON: Uh, um, my dad wouldn't let me eat junk food. Like I would get a candy bar every once in a while, but he was kind of strict on that. Like sunflower seeds, I was never allowed to eat. Um, gum, I couldn't eat. I'd always have to sneak it. Um, candy didn't really play a factor in my life. Potato chips. Dorito's, Funyons, and so forth, but not a lot of candy.
>
> REESE: Um-huh.
>
> CAYLON: Not a lot of candy because I'm one of those like—I would always try to abuse candy. Like all the time I went to the store I would always steal candy. Like you know how they got the little candy thing and you can open up the little thing and then pick your own pounds of candy?
>
> REESE: Yeah.
>
> CAYLON: I would always go and pick a piece out and put it in my pocket. My dad would get all pissed off. "What did I tell you about eating candy? Your teeth are going to fall out." This and that. But my cousins, they had junk food galore.
>
> REESE: So going along with this topic. Why do you think your dad wasn't so open to you eating certain types of foods?
>
> CAYLON: Yeah, because growing up my dad like, they weren't—they didn't have that much money and he'd always eat junk food and by the time he said he was six years old, he had a row of silver teeth. They're all silver teeth right here. And he's always said like when I have a kid I'm never going to let them eat junk food at all in any shape, form, or fashion. So that sucked.

Although he acknowledged that he did not like the way his dad restricted his food, Caylon's parenting strategies around eating resembled those of his father. He too monitored his daughter's food intake:

> REESE: You told me about your childhood growing up and kind of presently what it's like in your home. You do most of the cooking, have changed the type of seasoning, don't eat a lot of pork. What do you offer your daughter in terms of food and eating?

CAYLON: Um, I don't give my daughter no candy neither just unless like when you grow up like that it's just like no, my kid ain't going to eat the same thing either.

REESE: How old is she?

CAYLON: Um, my daughter is 7, she'll be 8 this year. Um, she's never had a cavity. I make her floss and brush. Um, a lot of vegetables. She eats a lot of—she loves deer meat, goat. She—she loves lamb chops like she goes to the Outback and gets nothing but lamb chops. Um, she eats healthy though. She eats like a lot of peanuts. She [pause] for some reason she's a weird little girl because she likes almonds and walnuts.

REESE: Hmm.

CAYLON: But she don't like cashews. I'm like, you're crazy little girl [laughs]. I guess she sees my grandmother, she's always with my grandmother and my grandmother's like, like superly, superly like on health shit. Always eating banana chips. Always took her ginkgo biloba pills. Um, always took her zinc pills and all this other. She always has like a million and one pills to take in the morning and it's like not medication, it's like vitamins. She eats like crackers, boiled eggs, and toast in the morning. She follows like a strict diet and my daughter likes to do it with her.

REESE: Uh-huh.

CAYLON: Um, [my daughter] loves marshmallows. That's something I'll let her eat, marshmallows. Um, no dark soda at all. Um, that's pretty much it. But I just want her to be healthy. Like my daughter's like a big old geek. She likes getting stuff like that, so she's going to be really healthy.

Caylon discussed his daughter's health as part of a generational continuum. In addition to his father's parenting strategies influencing his choices surrounding his daughter's food consumption, so did his grandmother's. Fruits and vegetables were important factors in how participants define healthiness. Through an explanation of his grandmother being on her "health shit," Caylon expanded that definition, including dietary supplements, nuts, boiled eggs, and being on a "strict diet." Caylon welcomed these behaviors and preferences, as he considered them as contributions to his daughter's healthiness.

Dametria also wanted her children to have access to healthy food options. However, she discussed this in the context not only of healthiness but of budgeting:

REESE: How do you budget for groceries?

DAMETRIA: How do I budget? I still have to go over. I get food stamps, but I still go over because I have a 16-year-old. You have to think about that. I have a 16-year-old eats like a grown man.

REESE: [*Laughs*]. Yeah.

DAMETRIA: I, myself, I like to buy half-price stuff. I'm a budget shopper. I'm always using coupons, but I buy like crab legs, shrimp, steak, good quality stuff, fruits, vegetables. They higher than them meats. They're higher, but I want them for my children and for myself, so I'm going to get what I want to get, and I just have to pay extra money.

REESE: Yeah.

DAMETRIA: My kids love their fruits and vegetables. It's all about budgeting. My girlfriend and I, we were just talking yesterday about budgeting. I used to be so good with budgeting. I mean, I had at least . . . I had extra money, and I had just had my oldest son [at the time]. I had my little budget sheet and everything, but every month, had my budget sheet, had everything that comes out off my card, my check card, everything. Rent, car, insurance. All of that. I used to budget. I say we used to say, "After today, we going to get back on our budget."

REESE: Mmm-hmm [*affirmative*].

DAMETRIA: It's easier when you on a budget where you can see where your money's going, what you are putting out there, what you have to save. It's worth it. I was just in here doing it. Before I got in the shower, I was calculating how much I spent yesterday, and I spent $282 yesterday out at the mall because I had to pick out me some dresses for church, some stockings, and I bought the kids $172 worth of uniforms. Bought [my daughter] two pair of pants, a sports skirt, and two pair of sweat pants, a regular pair of pants, uniform pants, and sports skirt. I bought her three shirts. I bought [my son] two pair of pants, and I bought him two shirts.

REESE: Mmm-hmm [*affirmative*].

DAMETRIA: I bought him a uniform jacket so he won't have to wear his coat because it's springtime, so I bought him a jacket with the fleece in the inside. I bought him some new shoes to wear with his uniform. Yeah, I just gave [my oldest son] $100 yesterday so he can get him some stuff, but yeah, I'm just calculating everything up, and I was like I did feel pretty good. At least I know it was benefitting all of us.

REESE: Yeah.

DAMETRIA: I bought me a pair of shoes. Those were only five dollars, so it was buy one, get 50 percent off at Payless, so I bought [my son] a pair. I did good, and I'm happy because I know my money went to a good cause.

REESE: Yeah, yeah. On average a month, how much do you think you spend on groceries?

DAMETRIA: Mmm. Probably a good . . . I'd say a good $450 or even over that. It depends on what the kids want.

REESE: Mmm-hmm [*affirmative*].

DAMETRIA: Then sometimes my son, I still have to pack him lunches on Tuesday because he's allergic to seafood, and at the school on Tuesdays, it's fish. So then my daughter, she get jealous, so I have to pack hers too.

REESE: Out of about $450, how much of that is covered with food stamps?

DAMETRIA: How much do they give me? They cut mine down so much, because it used to be almost $600. Now it's $400. I just checked my card. It's like $472, so this month I'll probably still have to add some more, so probably a good five-something this month, but normally, I normally I get about six, but since my son is on disability, he gets a check, and he gets child support . . . It helps though. So like my money not going to waste, and I still have extra money sometimes at the end of the month, and I try to save some in case [the] kids want or need something.

Mr. Harris began talking about healthiness in the context of budgeting, making decisions about what to buy, and his own health concerns:

REESE: About how much do you spend on a weekly or monthly basis on groceries?

MR. HARRIS: Um, like $500 a month.

REESE: Mm-hmm.

MR. HARRIS: I would rather spend more because some of the stuff that I would like to get, nuts and raisins, it's a little bit more expensive. That's, that's basically it, but if I, I could live off . . . I could do chicken and rice a lot very well.

REESE: Mm-hmm.

MR. HARRIS: I can also do beans and rice, hamburgers. I usually, usually eat, uh, turkey burgers. So I could write a budget where I could survive and make it. But what happens is that you run out. No, you really don't have that, in my case, I really don't have actually enough as we would want. But you have enough to, you know, basically get along with, 'cause that's what a parent does. That's on me.

REESE: Yeah.

MR. HARRIS: And so, uh, that's basically my challenge.

REESE: Hmm.

MR. HARRIS: Yeah. Uh, and so I can't even get my, uh, dental work done so, you know, we have all these things on the personal level. What you have is you have your food and you have your medical care. If, if you have to save on food 'cause you have a lot of kids then you may not eat the most nutritional things because eating right is expensive and you have to be practical.

Dametria and Mr. Harris each discussed their children's food wants and needs within a context of being fiscally responsible. Dametria was adamant that—even though fruits and vegetables cost more—she would get what was best for her children, even it meant supplementing her food budget. Mr. Harris, on the other hand, placed more emphasis on the type of negotiations necessary within budgetary constraints. While he desired to eat healthier because he believed it to be beneficial, his dental health suffered because of it. At the time of the interview, Mr. Harris was missing almost all his front teeth. "Being practical" about how to spend his money meant sometimes choosing between buying healthier food options and paying for medical care.

Daron acknowledged and challenged the myth that people do not want to eat healthy. In doing so, he implicitly assigned some blame to the realities of limited options and the stores that serve the neighborhood. This counters or at least contextualizes individual responsibility by suggesting that preferences are not the problem. The supply is the problem:

It's not that people don't want to eat healthy. I drive to international markets and stuff, because I've got kids and I want organic food, and I'm not going to get it here. This Safeway is horrible now. It used to be good. Now, for a lot of different reasons I don't even care to explore, it's not. I don't go shopping there. They don't ever have . . . [pause] my palette is different. I'm just not going to eat fried chicken and french fries. I can't even get fresh cut carrots; you know what I'm saying? Stuff I can get at an international market. I'll drive out and get it.

In the same breath, though, Daron turned to a racialized discourse about healthy eating by juxtaposing "fried chicken and french fries" with "fresh carrots." Fried chicken has long been linked with racialized understandings of African American foodways that are limited, degrading, and reflective of anti-Blackness in food discourse. Here, Daron evokes this reference as a way of distancing himself from that type of "unhealthy" eating and, by extension, the store he perceives as one that perpetuates it instead of offering fresh carrots. In this case, discourses about healthiness are tied directly to not only Daron's experiences and preferences but also space and access.

Conclusion

This chapter has explored critiques residents had of their local shopping choices, the alternatives to the local Safeway that they incorporated into their food geographies, and the significance of understanding Black residents' preferences as part of a larger conversation about food access inequities. For the residents who lived in Deanwood specifically and in Ward 7 broadly, the ways that race and racialization shaped neighborhood food systems had implications not only for their shopping patterns but also for the quality of the stores and critiques offered for those that did not meet their expectations. Even for residents who had cars or economic stability, meeting their needs outside the neighborhood came with a considerable cost, at least in terms of time and potentially in terms of additional dollars spent. For those in economically precarious positions and without cars, the costs associated with grocery shopping were high, as considerations were not solely about the type or amount of food available but also about the amount of stress associated with shopping and decisions made based on access to transportation. Across the board, residents were clear: they understood the disparities they faced, they were equipped with knowledge and tools (sometimes limited) to navigate these disparities, and they had little or no expectation that stores that did not meet their expectations would change.

When it comes to how race and racialization shape food shopping experiences, much of the focus has been on whiteness and the alternative food movement, demonstrating the ways in which white, presumably middle-class values shape shopping spaces to the exclusion of Black shoppers. Yet, a considerable amount remains unknown about what Black shoppers desire in a shopping experience and the extents to which they go to meet those desires. As demonstrated by survey and interview responses, Black residents have high expectations for grocery shopping experiences, and those expectations—depending on access to resources—take them beyond their neighborhood boundaries to find stores that meet their needs.

In this way, Black residents were not waiting for others to improve the local food system by way of supermarkets, farmers' markets, or community gardens. Some did express a desire for more options. However, there was not an expectation that they would be available anytime soon, for a variety of reasons. Perhaps as a reflection of ongoing, contentious relationships with the state and corporations, they expressed criticisms of the local food environment while at the same time indicating little or no hope that corporate interests or practices would change. Instead, they created food geographies that reflected how multilayered structural inequities influenced the contours of accessing food. In addition, these food geographies reflected the extents to which Black residents were not simply attempting to meet basic needs but were interested in finding food resources that met their shopping and preference expectations. Much of the literature on food access in Black neighborhoods misses this point: that Black residents operate in a way that demonstrates their understanding that meeting basic, everyday needs is only the bare minimum.

As these residents navigated structural food inequities, their food geographies demonstrated that expectations and preferences were not merely individual preferences ascribed to specific people or stores. Instead, they were also spatial, inscribed in the foodscape, and offered additional social commentary on the extent to which food inequities constrain choices but do not unequivocally dictate the decisions residents make. This is one of the many problems with the food desert metaphor and narrative: its application presupposes that residents are passive consumers who are trapped. Instead, even when their choices are constrained, residents demonstrate that thought and action go into not only critiquing their immediate foodscape but also into informing the ways they seek options to meet their various needs. Even for poor residents, there is a degree to which they transgress the boundaries of food inequities that constrain them.

Studies on food consumption preferences have largely been limited to taste, reflecting a theoretical interest in the ways in which cultural patterns and class are reflected in and reproduced in what people eat. These studies have largely focused on the individual, which allows researchers to see patterns in cultural consumption. Raphaël Charron-Chénier argues that individualistic approaches to researching consumption offer very little insight into the role of consumption in the reproduction of social inequality.[20] When applied specifically to food and grocery stores, mapping and understanding residents' preferences tell us something not only about their agency, but also about the extent to which they can leverage economic, social, and cultural capital to meet their needs, inadvertently reproducing the very social inequities that many critique.

CHAPTER THREE

What Is Our Culture? I Don't Even Know

Nostalgia and Memory in Evaluations of Food Access

> They've forgotten what their responsibility is. It's not for you to
> benefit. Your job is to hold up and pull up, not to live on top of.
> I don't know when that happened. I don't know when that culture
> shift happened or what generation is responsible for it. We don't
> even talk about it. It's such a difficult place. This is what the
> community is, so your food desert is a result. *What is our culture?*
> *I don't even know.*
>
> —DARON

Primarily concerned with the ways unequal food access is socially produced, chapters 1 and 2 examined national shifts in spatial and cultural
food practices, paying attention to how racial residential segregation,
community-based food production and distribution, and supermarkets'
growing monopoly influenced and factored into residents' strategies for
navigating the food landscape. As George Lipsitz argues, "The racial projects
of U.S. society have always been spatial projects."[1] As the previous chapters
explore, food is not exempt from but deeply embedded in these spatial projects. This chapter examines how memory and nostalgia factor into how
residents understand and critique their neighborhood food system. Using
nostalgia as a framework for understanding connections residents make between the past and the present, this chapter explores the loss of and the
desire to reclaim a foodscape and a configuration of community (imagined
and otherwise) as components of residents' engagement with procuring
food.

We create and critique worlds through stories we tell about the past. These
stories are not only interpersonal creations between the storyteller and the
listener but also spatial, reflecting relationships between people, space, and
time. Just as neighborhood boundaries are permeable, as shown in the previous chapter, so too are the socially constructed barriers between past, present, and future. Writing about Octavia Butler's *Kindred*, Katherine McKittrick
argues that "blackness becomes a site of radical possibility, supernatural trav-
els, and difficult epistemological returns to the past and the present. Butler

presents us with landscapes shaped by selves and experiences that are extraordinary in that they are not comfortably situated in the past, present, or future. The landscape is neither complete nor fully intelligible."[2] These memories and nostalgia also inspire embodied practice. Offering "productive nostalgia" as an analytical frame, Lorena Munoz argues that the nostalgic imaginaries employed by food vendors not only create the conditions for them to have a stable clientele but also become avenues through which consumers are reminded of home, putting vendors in a position to perform emotional labor that requires managing consumers' memories and emotions.[3] Productive nostalgia is defined as "a process in which nostalgia is not just memories or imaginations but instead calls for the embodiment and enactment of practice."[4]

Some residents I interviewed drew directly from their own experiences with changes in the local foodscape and their familial foodways over time. Others, particularly middle-aged participants, drew on stories they had heard from others and their understanding of African American histories of struggle and self-determination. Whether they had personally experienced Deanwood with more robust food options was inconsequential to the articulations and circulation of narratives about a decline in self-reliance and racial solidarity. In these narratives, the presumed connectedness of residents in Black neighborhoods was key, and that ideal structured residents' understandings of challenges to Black life and food access. When residents reflected on Deanwood's food past, it was not white supremacy, racial inequity, or segregation that characterized their stories. Instead, it was abundance, choice, and community cohesiveness.

Memories of and stories about the past combined with residents' present experiences with unequal food access and their ideas about the future to create nostalgic imaginaries. Imaginaries, including spatial ones, are used in social science research to capture how discourses, stories, media, and images circulate to create representations of people or places that are not necessarily built on experience or observable fact but have material implications for how people relate to the spaces in question.[5] These imaginaries are racialized and spatialized, as Black experiences with enslavement, Jim Crow, residential segregation, educational inequities, and anti-Black policing reflect ongoing policies and practices that produce different outcomes for Black people. Focusing on Black people's engagement with space despite the ways white supremacy attempts to curtail life and movement, Lipsitz defines the Black spatial imaginary as the antithesis of the white spatial imaginary, which is defined in part by segregated neighborhoods and schools and greater access to amenities. The Black spatial imaginary, produced through the ways Black people negotiate power, space, and confinement to create places of care and celebration, reflects "a socially-shared understanding of the importance of public space and its power to shape opportunities and life chances."[6] How does a socially shared understanding of food access and responsibility come to bear on how residents articulate what they have lost and how they understand the consequences of not being self-reliant? Through analyses of nostalgia, a yearning for something past that is no longer recoverable,[7] this chapter examines how the presence and absence of food institutions become consequential not only in residents' foodways but also in how they have re/imagined community through a lens of formerly cohesive Black neighborhoods.

"It Was a Community. Okay?"

Cliff was in transition when I met him. The environmental justice organization he founded had just received notice that they no longer had office space in the building they had rented for years. "Part of the many changes happening around here," he said as he noticed me taking in the boxed-up books and paintings and posters resting against the baseboards of the walls, waiting for a new home. He did not need to explain what he meant by changes. I knew that he was referring to gentrification in Ward 7. We sat in chairs next to each other while Cliff did most of the talking. During our first meeting, I mused at the jarring juxtaposition of the stories I had heard about him being a spitfire and his relatively small stature — perhaps no taller than 5′6″ — and his kind eyes.

Cliff Haynes was a sixty-four-year-old community leader who, after four years of college, moved back home after his father encouraged him to do so. Allured by homeownership without owing a mortgage, Cliff moved into the house his family built in Deanwood after they migrated to Washington, D.C., from South Carolina in 1940. LeDroit Park had been their first stop because, like others, they were looking for a thriving Black center. However, his father hated the neighborhood, and after discovering the area east of the Anacostia River, settled in Deanwood. Cliff was the youngest sibling and the only one born in Deanwood, entering this world on the living room floor of the house his parents built. His early years in that home and Deanwood informed Cliff's understandings of community, choice, and cohesion.

As he talked, it was clear that Cliff not only loved the neighborhood and community but was also troubled by transitions he witnessed throughout his life. He talked about change from the first words he uttered, and after he discussed Deanwood more broadly, I asked him to shift the focus to food in the neighborhood. He responded at length:

> When I was a child growing up, there were four grocery stores within a four-block radius here. Four, I mean, and I'm not talking about the corner delis. I'm saying grocery stores. There was a Grand Union, there was a Safeway, there was a Giant, there was an A&P, all within this corridor. It was very much a choice. This was a vibrant shopping area right here. Maybe commercial [corridor]. This community had no reason to really go outside of it unless they just decided to. It was that kind of a community. There were at least that many banks in this community as well. There were drugstores across the street from one another. Standard was on one corner. People's, which changed to CVS, was on the other, diagonally across the street from one another. Yes, that was all right here in this commercial [corridor]. Then, you had what they called the D.G.S. stores, the district grocery stores. They all had delis in them, so you could get cold cut meats. Yes, they made sandwiches in those places. All of those were scattered within the communities, which have now turned into these places that sell mostly beer, wine and junk, occupying those same buildings. They operated as a real community enterprise, too, because they worked with the people who lived in the communities. My mom would write a note and give it to me and say, "Okay, take this around to Alvin's Market." I'd take that note in there and I'd give it to guy sitting behind the counter. He said, "Oh, you Miss Hayne's boy." He'd go, get this, get that, put it in the bag and give it to me. I didn't have any money. What she would do is pay him when she got [some money] . . . They had, that was the kind of relationship he had with the community. It was a real community. That's why I say more so than neighborhood. It was a community. Okay?

Cliff's "okay?" was rhetorical. He neither expected me to ask a follow-up nor thought I would not understand what he meant by "it was a community." Indeed, from other parts of his narrative, my own study of African American communities, and other neighbors' reflections on the past, I knew what he meant by "it was a community." Cliff was referring to a cohesive, predominantly Black space in which people knew each other well, got along well, and looked out for each other. As if to prove his point about what it meant to be a community that valued everyone, despite economic hierarchies, Cliff explained:

> Sitting around here, that's the way [it was] and it didn't matter. Two things that I remember. Now, there was, I guess what some would call a few homeless people but there wasn't nothing to the extent that it is now. These folks really weren't homeless. They just didn't have their own place. They would stay with somebody. A lot of times, it would only be for periods of time but it wasn't like they were sleeping out on a bench. Folks didn't . . . they would look out for folks like that. They just looked out for them. There was this one guy. We used to, we were cruel but he would do work for folks, [and they would] give him a few dollars and so forth. He stayed in the basement next door to where I lived. He stayed in the basement with the older son of the people who lived there. They shared a placed down in the basement. Yes. We used to mess with him, make him say things. He'd be talking to us. We'd . . . But that was . . . Nobody was doing anything harmful.

Though Cliff himself never mentions racism, anti-Blackness, or policies and practices that constrained the movement of Black people in the District, they were the backdrop against which the thriving commercial corridor he described existed. As discussed in previous chapters, the ways in which anti-Blackness shaped neighborhoods, and by extension food access, largely defined not only Black entrepreneurship, but Jewish and white folks' relationships to the neighborhood as well. Paul Mullins argued that anti-Black politics, residential segregation, and white control of much public space congealed in such a way that Black folks found their footing in the American dream as entrepreneurs and consumers.[8] This created what Bobby Wilson called a "separate black economy" that fueled social and political spaces separate from those that excluded them.[9] In Cliff's storytelling, the makeup of the community, as distinct from the neighborhood, was possible in part because people's needs were met without having to go too far, which contributed to the rapport that people built with each other and the store owners. Food stores as well as informal food economies were as significant to the social fabric of Deanwood as churches and schools.

The self-sufficiency Cliff described was contingent on both the food resources available and a sociocultural fabric in which intimate relationships among community members were integral to maintaining a safe space. Changes in the food landscape had consequences for the sociocultural fabric of Deanwood. Cliff's narrative underscores how the spatiality of grocery stores is not simply about where the stores are located. The present is filtered through a host of experiences that people have had, including experiences with stores that no longer exist. These experiences come to bear on how people consider the present, how they evaluate it, and how they navigate it.

Many people like Cliff brought up community in their interviews. Residents believed there was a different (better) way to be and relate to each other. Conversations about food retail evoked this. In most cases, as explored later in this chapter, the lack of food retail was framed as a community responsibility or failure. The self-reliance narrative that runs through Cliff's and many other interviews suggests that it is not only about procuring food but also about creating a sustainable community in which people maintain intimate relationships with store owners and among each other, a theme that also runs through alternative food movements, though Black communities after often only marginally integrated into mainstream movements.

"It's Just Changed So Much"

Anne and I sat in the living room of her childhood home. Anne was a retired schoolteacher who substitute taught part time. We sat across from each other, and I visually took in as much of her home as possible: a multistory house that she lived in alone, neatly decorated with black-and-white photos and plants. From the living room, I could see through the kitchen to catch a glimpse of the backyard that once held her mother's garden, which had long been overgrown. During her childhood, Anne's mother grew squash, cucumbers, and tomatoes. She also tended a peach tree, the fruit of which she used to make peach wine. "Do you garden now?" I asked. "I'm afraid to put anything out in that garden now. There was a snake back there!" She laughed and shook her head. The mention of the snake triggered the memory about how her mother acquired the peach tree in the backyard: "I'm trying to think, what other food? What other food? But you reminded me . . . the food. And I remember the peach tree, they got it from over here in the wooded area, and a snake was wrapped around it when they got it. I remember saying, 'Oh, what's that? You're not going to bring that snake in here!'" Like Cliff, Anne inherited her home from her parents and had a relationship with the neighborhood that spanned several decades. "We were really self-contained," she remembered. "But once the older people passed on, and the children would come back . . . I basically have been here for the most part. But the children would come back and unfortunately, they didn't always want to keep up the properties." As a nearly lifelong Deanwood resident, Anne had deep connections to the neighborhood and other residents. Before I began with interview questions, Anne asked me where I grew up. "I'm from Texas. A very small town in Texas," I said. "Where in Texas?" she asked. "Crockett. It's a small town in east Texas. Only seven thousand people." "Oh, that's small. Yeah!" she exclaimed and chuckled. I laughed too and said, "Yes, small. Everybody was connected in some kind of way." Though much had changed, as Cliff noted and as Anne herself would articulate, elder residents in Deanwood retained a proprietary relationship to the neighborhood and the stories told about it. As such, when I interviewed elders, they often wanted to know about me and where I was from. I took this to mean they wanted to make sure their memories, their stories, and their community were safe with me.

Anne's nodding and smile indicated that she approved of my small-town upbringing and perhaps thought I would understand the power of intimate connections between neighbors. This prompted Anne to consider who and what rooted her in Deanwood. As Anne talked, it was clear that most of her close relationships in the neighborhood reflected her own status. She herself was educated, having acquired a master's degree, and as she spoke of her neighbors, signifiers of their social class peppered the brief introductions she provided me:

ANNE: I was going to give you the names of a couple other people, if you're interested. Like the lady on the corner, whose house you parked very close to, just as you go around the corner on the right-hand side. She was here when I was born.

REESE: Oh, wow!

ANNE: And so was the man next door, but he has a lot of health issues. But [the lady on the corner] she might talk with you, and her daughter and I are about the same age. So all of us have been here, for primarily most of our lives . . . You're talking about people in their sixties who are pretty vital, because I mean, I was going to go buy a condominium but that fell through. Oh, and my second grade best friend just passed in May, and lived around the corner. She was an astrophysicist. She had a master's. Yeah, and her sister actually has a degree. We can tell you some stories about how hard it was when we were coming through to even get a master's degree back then, even in Black universities.

REESE: Hmmmm [affirmative].

ANNE: But anyway, there might be another person up around the
corner who I can refer you to, if that's what you want.
REESE: Sure. If people want to talk and share, I'm willing to listen.
ANNE: Let me give you these names. [Name deleted] . . . and he had
two sons to grow up around here. One son has a PhD and has just
moved to Kentucky. His wife has a PhD in school psychology and she
came down from New Jersey or somewhere. And the other son has a
law degree from Catholic. He's in his thirties. [Name deleted] is in
his sixties, about sixty-five I think. Then you have the lady on the
corner, she's in her nineties. Her daughter is around my age. I'm
sixty-four. I think she's sixty-four or sixty-five. I can give you these
numbers too. There is a lady who is in her seventies, about seventy-
five, seventy-six, who works for Safeway. And she lives right around
the corner from where you just were.

Though Deanwood was economically and socially diverse, there was very
little contact across social class. As Karyn Lacy and Mary Pattillo note, Black
people may occupy the same neighborhoods and still have different social
worlds and different priorities, even if they portray racial solidarity.[10] The
mention of Anne's neighbor who worked at Safeway was a transition point
in our conversation. I mentioned that it would be an added interesting perspective to talk with someone who worked for the store and also lived in
Deanwood. Anne responded, "It would be such a big different perspective
from somebody, because she's Black, but I tell you, people got big opinions
about Safeway." I encouraged her to continue. After a pause she said, "Well,
I'm not fond of them because once in the seventies, and once in the nineties, so Safeway said that they were just perking up their place. And next
thing I knew, they were selling it. Well, leasing it or what have you. That's
when Super Pride, which was Black-owned, came through." "Is the temperature okay?" she asked. It was September, and by D.C. standards still
very warm outside. "No, no, it's fine. I'm comfortable," I said. "Okay, I just
wanted to make sure. Sometimes I'm cold and other people are burning up!"
    Picking up the conversation, Anne directed me across the street, where
an empty space stood between her home and a church. The church used to
be a Safeway before it closed in 1980, and then Super Pride before it too
closed. Partially fenced, the space held nothing. The bakery of her childhood
was gone. So too was the baseball field. It was empty. But for Anne, it held
memories. It was the place where her family unearthed the peach tree that
they eventually planted in their backyard. I tried to imagine the green grass

where Anne and her friends played baseball. I wondered what the bread smelled like that she and her family bought for less than a dollar from the nearby bakery. I looked at the field and tried to imagine the space filled with the physical representations of Anne's memories. "Across the street" was a cultural, symbolic, and temporal marker as much as it was a spatial one. Memories of "across the street" stood in stark contrast to the present-day emptiness.

As Anne continued to talk about Safeway, her narrative, much like Cliff's, was riddled with references to past grocery stores and also to restaurants. Anne's use of the present-day Safeway as a catalyst for discussing stores and restaurants that were no longer in business reveals the ways in which the contemporary foodscape triggered memories of the past:

ANNE: Okay . . . Safeway, which became Super Pride . . . it made us so mad because I'd been going to Safeway, I would say from the time I was about ten or so. This over here initially was just woods when I was a little girl. And then, by the time I was about eight years old, a bakery bought the area, and so where you see the fence out there, there was no fence around it. And where that church is on the other side, I'm sure a million people have told you, that was where the Safeway was in this neighborhood. And so you could go back and forth and buy groceries and do things. I know that for $25, I could get a big . . . you know several bags . . . big bags with steaks and all kinds of things. And now $25 . . . That's why I go to Wegman's so I can get $5 off of $25.

But first there was Spic N Span, which was a Jewish-owned store, right here on the corner of Division and Nannie Helen Burroughs. Of course, you have to understand, in those days, you had blue laws, so nothing was open on Sundays. There may have been a drugstore open and you could only get aspirin or something like that. And it's just changed so much. We had several High's, have you ever heard of High's?

REESE: No.

ANNE: High's was an ice cream store . . . dairy store. And they sold ice cream, milk. I'm sure they sold bread, but that wasn't their primary function. It was like the Baskin Robbins but on steroids, because they literally had stores everywhere. I understand that they still do have stores in other small outreach locations. So there was one right here on Nannie Helen Burroughs, almost next to Sargent. Because there was a house that's between, I think High's and Sargent. Where you see the parking lot, there was a major fire, so I think part of that was where a house was, right over there. Then they were robbed a number of times and a Black[-owned] record store moved in. Of course when Safeway moved in, of course Spic N Span met its demise.

REESE: Yeah.

ANNE: I was a real little girl then . . . I wasn't there. I do not remember that much, because of course . . . Spic N Span was right here on the corner. Now I have another neighbor who you could talk to. She swears that there was a Chinese carryout out around here. I don't remember 'til I got older, because I just never got much of the carryout. I was in my fifties before I even realized that carryout was around the corner. I remember Barnett's being at what is now Marvin Gaye or what's it called? Fitch Place? I think it's Marvin Gaye, right at the corner. If you want me to, I can drive you around to show you where some of the spots were. You know where the Marvin Gaye Park is?

REESE: Yes.

ANNE: That store right there on the corner, it was Barnett's Carry-out. But I believe at one time before it became Barnett's, that was one of the original drugstores in the area, and then Division Drugs moved up here next to the gas station.

REESE: Okay.

ANNE: A lot of the stores . . . well, back to Safeway. After Safeway sold, Super Pride came in. Well, you could tell that the refrigeration was already going bad; you could still get that same scent. And by the time they flipped it over to the Asian store, it still had that scent and I think eventually they probably went out of business because of that. And then the church came, and I think the church probably came in the late nineties or sometime like that. Our unfortunate thing is that a lot of places that I want to say that were stores or might have been businesses, became churches. It's ironic because, of course, and it's not that that church doesn't do good for the community. They bury, that church is known for burying a number of people that you hear that are killed and don't have money or means or anyone. And they do bury people; you'll see if you ever go in there you'll see it all over the walls all the people they've buried. But if you really think it's really a food desert. Of course you could get chitlins. I didn't start really eating chitlins and pig feet until I was really in my twenties and then

I stopped. Then I became a vegetarian. Then I . . . Right now,
I'm not a vegetarian, but I try to eat pretty healthy.

Neither Cliff nor Anne was simply talking about the loss of stores. Their narratives reveal the interconnectedness between the loss of stores, community cohesiveness, and ultimately, self-reliance. In both cases, these losses—or remembering stores and practices from the past that no longer exist—were contextualized by nationwide policy and cultural changes that affected residents' lives at the neighborhood and family levels. Desegregation, or the process through which Black people now legally had access to places and things that had previously been denied them, was one such political change that came up in interviews, particularly as residents reflected on how the cultural geography and spatiality of food changed in the wake of increased opportunity. I never explicitly asked about integration during formal or informal interviews, though it is not surprising that it came up. Michelle Boyd argues that the reimagining of Jim Crow as a racial utopia absent the racial trauma that accompanied it functions as a political and social framing through which Black residents and leaders design projects through urban renewal programs.[11]

Anne tried to name Black-owned businesses in the neighborhood and struggled to do so. In the middle of thinking about businesses that existed in the present, Anne interrupted her own thought with, "I will just say it and many of my friends say this, that integration helped to destroy some of the communities. There was more pride . . . people were proud of what they had. Once they were able to go to Brightwood, and once they were able to go to, you know, other places . . . Of course, Georgetown did the opposite thing. The people from Georgetown were tossed to the southeast. Some of them came this way." In a follow-up interview, Anne's response was not as passionate as in the previous one, though she reiterated her earlier sentiment about the out-migration of residents to other neighborhoods. During this second discussion, however, she focused on those who stayed behind, connecting this explicitly to the development of new food retail:

Um, in a way, integration was good for blacks in this city, but in many areas middle-class blacks were able to move elsewhere. It sort of left those of us who stayed you know, uh, in a position that we were not used to. So we still don't have a real grocery store over here. Um, the Walmart that they're going to put up on East Capitol Street, they should have put it in our area first because they would have had the clientele that they were looking to really use their store. But they took it up town, took it on H Street with people who do not really utilize Walmart to the same extent that we would have because we do have public housing. Of course, we do also have a number of us over here that are black middle class who do not plan to move because it's not cost-effective at this time.

Unequal food landscapes create conditions under which corporations like Walmart are welcomed over the alternative—no store at all—despite the fact that they negatively impact small businesses. Anne's lament that the East Capitol Street Walmart was not the first to open in the city reflects the ongoing tensions created as a by-product of racial residential segregation and gentrification. In 2013, Walmart opened two of six planned stores in the District. These two stores opened in Wards 4 and 6. At the time, both wards had experienced consistent gentrification, and the Walmart openings were heralded as a way to keep the surrounding neighborhoods affordable for working-class residents. Prior to their opening, the District had no Walmart stores. Unlike Wards 4 and 6, Ward 7—where the East Capitol store would be located—had yet to experience similar shifts. The East Capitol store Anne referenced was one of the remaining four stores that were to open. However, in 2016, Walmart pulled out of the deal with the city to open that store, and in 2018 agreed to pay $1.3 million to the District of Columbia as a result.

The idea of being self-contained or self-reliant was a constant theme, and thus the challenges to this self-containment and reliance were also prominent in the residents' narratives. For the first half of Cliff's two-hour interview, he talked about the past and his memories. He reflected on being a boy who dug in the dirt while his mother gardened and on the stores that he remembered. When we continued, I shifted gears to unpack Cliff's perspectives on what had changed since the times of his mother's garden and his family's Sunday meals. I asked, "We've talked about stores, restaurants, traditions. What has changed?" To which he responded:

I think that what has changed more than anything else is things change people and when I say that, it's certain things that change the way that people function. Certain things that came about that became what was so-called convenient, caused people to not do some of the traditional things that they did like cook at home on a regular basis. Lifestyle also impacted how people function so everybody moving in and out at different times. Dads sitting down for dinner. We really tried to still do that. Right now, it's just my wife and I and I have a grandson that lives with me. You never can catch up with him. He always has something but we're really trying to at least sit down and have dinner.

I think that the pace of things, all of that had changed. When the change started to become apparent, I would say in the late sixties. Certain opportunities of various kind[s] opened up for people in these communities. Jobs, like with the passage of [the] Civil Rights bill in the early sixties and '64 had an impact.

I know my father, for example, he would hardly be around for dinner during the week because he worked the evening shift. He would be around Sunday and on the weekends but he worked the evening shift. But it was cool because I can remember eating breakfast with him all the time. He would come in, he would fix breakfast and I would sit down and eat breakfast with him. Yes, those things started to change how people function.

McDonald's, fast food. The opposite of that was what we had. We had slow food. Fast food had that impact. It changed things. McDonald's create[d] competition because Wendy's followed McDonald's and then that was easy for folks to run in and grab and go. That changed. Then, I think also, I think the sixties with the cultural revolution, that's what we went through. Black folks started looking at some of the things like farming and they looked at that as associated with that feeling of, "Oh, we're not slaves." I guess folks became too sophisticated to dig in the ground.

Cliff articulated changes in policies, people, and practices. The civil rights legislation of the 1960s has been the subject of much academic inquiry, particularly for those who questioned how the legislation translated into changing or influencing the everyday practices of people in communities. As Cliff alludes to here, he did not see the civil rights legislation as wholly positive, indicating that the opening up of opportunities had some unintended negative consequences for family and community life. The dream of integration and equal rights far outweighed the reality. A broken educational system, racial residential segregation, and documented discriminatory hiring practices persist, though there is legislation that supposedly regulates such practices. The results of this—the educational gap, unequal distribution of resources, and the wealth gap—were all concerns that my research participants navigated in one way or another. In Cliff's estimation, though, the legislation's influence—and its limitations—were not just structural. They were also communal.

Furthermore, Cliff reflects on the ways people and practices changed over time. He declares that "things change people." This very sentiment was communicated to a group of supermarket executives by Mary Gardiner Jones in 1967. Using the phrase "a revolution of rising expectations," Jones articulated that consumer culture was changing and that as part of that change, supermarket executives needed to pay more attention to how they would integrate Black people into their respective markets.[12] The changes that came with convenience—faster food, less frequent grocery runs, technological advancements in food production and preservation—were not without consequences. Convenience charted paths for consumers to ostensibly have shorter food preparation times and fewer trips to the grocery store, all while working longer hours. Yet these advancements, "things" in Cliff's words, had an impact on how people functioned. Both social progress and modernity required sacrifice—sacrificing an agricultural tradition and mealtimes as the central focus of family life.

The changes Cliff articulated are not positive, and they disrupted the family unit, for which the dinner table was a central component. The ways in which Cliff reminisced on his father working longer hours, having less time for dinner during the week but making time on the weekends, reflect a common narrative about U.S. families prior to "convenience": a heteronormative family unit that is maintained through gendered notions of labor, the backbone of which was the presence of a father whose hard work financially provided for the family so that the mother could either not work outside the home at all or not have to work full-time. Stephanie Coontz argues that self-reliance is one of the most cherished American values and that families in the United States tend to overstate the self-sufficiency of the family unit, which was often maintained through unequal gender roles.[13]

As Cliff continued to talk, the gender roles he remembered from his family continued to unfold under the banner of tradition. He reflected on his mother, who was a stay-at-home mother and wife:[14]

As the older folks, most of these people came from the South. They came with a tradition. I know both of my parents were from South Carolina. They came with that tradition. I tell folks this and folk say, "You remember back that far?" Look, I can remember when I was a little kid, I mean when I say a little kid, it was [before] going to school, okay? My mom would be out gardening. I was always digging in the dirt. I remember that, because one of the things is I would get smacked on the hand for putting it in my mouth. I remember her, it seems like she was always gardening. There was like, in the morning, it was like part of the early routine. Working out, yes, gardening.

We had, now this is very interesting. We ate fresh for the most part. I remember when we got our first refrigerator. I was, that was just before I became a teenager. We got our first refrigerator. We were all fascinated by it . . . But prior to that, we had an ice box and the ice box was out on the back porch. I wish we kept that thing. I'd like to have that now. It was porcelain interior and it was made out of wood. For the most part, they only kept things like milk, butter, eggs, it wasn't a storage place for leftovers like these refrigerators are.

What wound up happening was, we ate fresh daily. She used to grow stuff. I'm going to tell you, I would eat corn out of that cornfield. We'd be out playing and rather than come home, we'd go to the cornfield and we'd break off some of that white corn. We'd shuck it down, get all that silk off, and we sit there and we eat a couple of ears of corn. It was good. Eat it just right just like that. People say, "Why you eat corn?" Look, it was sweet and [my friend] would come and we would sit down and nobody could see us in the cornfield, because if we came home, they'd find something for you to do or something. That was how it was. That was how it was over here. Was it like the country? Yes, it was the country in the city.

Cliff connected spatial changes in food, cultural changes in consumerism, and changing familial structures to make a case that structural changes in the food system had individual- and family-level consequences. But his narrative also heavily depended on gendered notions of work, most notably his mother's garden as a site for both feeding her family and performing acceptable (ideal) womanhood. This was not uncommon in interviews, particularly those with men who tended to reflect on their mothers and grandmothers as ideal archetypes of womanhood. Daron, for example, described the women in his family as "the classic African American strong black women" and said that these women barely exist anymore.

The nostalgic food imaginaries he and Anne articulated also relied on sameness in the construction of a past that was much better than the present, one characterized not only by racial sameness but also by the absence of class conflict or difference and by a gendered order to maintaining family and community life. Processes such as desegregation disrupted this sameness (or the illusion of sameness), because those with most access to social and economic capital made different decisions about where to live, where to hang out, and with whom to socialize. In this way, desegregation was as much a process about remaking space as it was about access.

"We Were Known as a Self-Reliant Community"

Janice, Koti, and I sat at a small table in the back room of The Coupe, a restaurant in the Columbia Heights neighborhood. Janice had suggested the place when I e-mailed her about setting up an interview. She and her husband arrived before me. She sent me a quick e-mail: "I'll be there with my husband. I have glasses and black shirt. Short black hair. I had a wisdom tooth taken out yesterday so excuse my puffy face. You can interview my husband as well. When you come in go right. Look left. We are all the way in the back by the couches." I found them in the back where she promised. Janice, a short, stout woman, stood to greet me with a hug, even though this was our first time meeting. Her husband, Koti—a tall, husky, bearded man— sat across from us. The Coupe was one of the newer restaurants in gentrified Columbia Heights. On that Friday morning we each ordered breakfast and five-dollar lattes, and sat and talked about Deanwood for an hour before Kofi left for work. Both Janice and Koti worked in creative industries. At the time, she had recently finished a project about Deanwood, highlighting the stories and faces of residents throughout the neighborhood to foster community pride and cohesion. Koti was a DJ and a rapper who had enjoyed success throughout D.C. and beyond. As we talked and ate, the irony of meeting in gentrified Columbia Heights instead of Deanwood was not lost on any of us.

Janice and Koti had lived in Deanwood for six years at the time of the interview and were deeply invested in not only the neighborhood structures but also the close-knit feel of the community that was a combination of myth and fading reality. In the middle of discussing Deanwood's growth and progress, Janice empathically asked: "We were known as a self-reliant community, like nobody is helping us. I mean I wasn't there, but you know. Like years ago they weren't being helped, just like now. So what did you do? Built your own homes and had general farms and made your own food, like you relied on each other. *Where is that?*" (emphasis added). This meeting with Janice and Koti was one where the ways of navigating their community—the physical, the social, and the cultural—collided. Laced with ideas of racial cohesion, economic concerns, and physical constraints, the past was an overlay in Janice's declaration and question, with self-reliance as the tie that bound. Janice's statement reflected the theme that ran throughout Anne's and Cliff's narratives: pride in the historical development of the neighbor-hood that has yielded high homeownership rates and families that have lived there for two and three generations, and also dismay about the current con-ditions. Daron expressed sentiments similar to Janice's: "We had little gar-dens everywhere. All of us had gardens back then. We didn't have all the amenities, but we were a community. The best part was we had other sys-tems that worked that don't work anymore. For instance, you could buy shoes in this community. You could get your hair cut. There were barter systems, and community-based systems that supported us thirty years ago, that don't exist anymore." Collectively, Janice's and Daron's words demonstrate that the elders did not have a monopoly on nostalgia. On the contrary, young entrepreneurs and community leaders like Janice and Daron were drawn to stories of Deanwood's early history when express-ing frustration about its current lack of progress or cohesiveness. Food became a marker of this, a barometer used to measure the strength of com-munity ties. Just as Anne's "across the street" was more than a spatial ref-erence, Janice's question was more than a rhetorical one. "Where is that?" pointed to an emptiness similar to the lot across the street from Anne's home. "Where is that?" was a question about searching, about emptiness, about lack. Coupled with Daron's statement about systems that no longer exist, the result is a base of residents for whom self-reliance is a strong cul-tural logic and platform but who question its existence in the present day.

These tensions are in part a by-product of the dissonance produced between individuals pursuing success and stability in a nation in which structural barriers ensure that achieving them is difficult for Black people. While Coontz rightfully acknowledges that public aid and safety nets have always existed and that individual achievement is largely a myth for all Americans,[15] the reality of Black life in the United States often includes her-alding individual achievement as a way toward upward mobility while also embracing it as a mechanism through which collective well-being can be achieved. The hope, then, is not solely in individual merit, but also in the potential for collective uplift and resistance, despite the failures of the state and corporations inherent in racial capitalism.

Cliff, Anne, and others of their generation saw glimpses of the American Dream's potential as their parents, grandparents, and neighbors settled in D.C., their version of the promised land after leaving the Deep South. But for younger residents, those in their thirties and forties who had been pushed to *make something out of themselves*, their experiences of urban life could best be described as what Marcus Hunter and Zandria Robinson called "the deferred dreams of the Great Migration": persistent segregation, income inequity and poverty, and unequal access to resources, including food.[16] For these residents, the nostalgic imaginaries concerning the benefits of self-reliant communities in terms of food were built not so much on experience as on the strength of memories and, even when critical, a belief in Black people's institution-building capacity. Regardless of their length of stay in Deanwood, some residents were clear that they saw one of the strengths of the neighborhood as its history of self-reliance (no matter how manufactured that history or narrative may have been) and that loss of it was a major blow to Deanwood's stability.

Racialized Responsibility

"Can I suggest something?" A man entering the building gestured toward my bag, which I had haphazardly left sitting on the ground beside me. I was sitting on the steps with Dametria, who had agreed to meet me outside her apartment. She lived in the housing projects that residents were being relocated from so that the units could be torn down and rebuilt. Because of their location on the outskirts of Deanwood proper, those who lived in the housing projects often considered themselves a separate community, although historically, others had considered them one and the same. The thirty-two-year-old mother of three was involved in her community. She attended the housing authority meetings, and her youngest children participated in the community garden in the projects.

"Mhmm," I mumbled, waiting for him to go on. "Why don't you take your pocketbook and put it in the middle?" I picked up my bag and put it on the concrete between Dametria and myself. "Right here?" "Yeah. Somebody could walk up and . . ." I interrupted him before he could finish. "There's no wallet in there so . . . but thank you." He nodded to us and kept walking, and I turned back to Dametria. She had lived in the housing projects for fourteen years, sometimes with a car, but carless at the time of the interview. "You have to look at it also, okay, you're—." Another person pushed past us into the building. "How you doin'?" she asked. I responded, "Good. How you doin'?" Dametria exchanged pleasantries as well, complimenting the woman on her outfit, and jumped back into her discussion of race and responsibility:

> DAMETRIA: You know, you have the Caucasians, their kids go out of
> their neighborhoods and care about where they shop at, so of course,

they're going to fight for getting these things, necessary stores for them to shop at. Here, us African Americans, a lot of us don't fight for it, you see what I'm saying?

REESE: Yeah.

DAMETRIA: It's like [Black people] don't care. They think things are supposed to be just given to them. Just like the Caucasians work hard, we have to do the same thing also . . . but do you see a lot of people in this African American neighborhood?

REESE: Yeah.

DAMETRIA: Do you see what I'm saying? If you go up to Georgetown, Northwest, Columbia Heights or somewhere up in that area where it's predominantly Caucasian, they take care of their things, and they participate and volunteer. You don't get a lot of African Americans to do that. It's sad to say.

REESE: Yeah.

DAMETRIA: Then they always say, "Well, the Caucasians this, the Caucasians that." Caucasians gave us opportunities. They have even given us free money. They're still in school. They further their education. We stop at a point. I mean, you just have to look at it. I tell people all the time, you cannot blame the Caucasian people for your mistakes. It's your mistakes.

REESE: Yeah.

DAMETRIA: I said, "I'm not mad at them." I said, "They building all around."

REESE: All around.

DAMETRIA: They had the money, they credit is good, they invest. Why are we complaining? You all don't even want to come to meetings around here, and you wonder why we're not getting funded?

REESE: Yeah, because they're slowly moving everybody out, right?

DAMETRIA: Exactly, and then it's close to being closed down, but like I say, the money's been taken away. A lot of people are not showing up at the meetings, so the outcome is what we get.

REESE: Mmm.

DAMETRIA: The other residents that do attend the meetings, we're getting frustrated because we're attending, but we're suffering because we're not getting a larger outcome at the meeting.

Though Dametria knew I was there to interview her about her experiences with food around and outside the neighborhood, that is not where she chose to start. She opened with this discussion of responsibility, which she described in racial terms. Dametria argued that Black people don't fight for anything, alluding to the idea that if they wanted more access to stores, it was on them to demand it. Ironically, the very housing projects she lived in were once inhabited by soldiers—those returning from World War II who needed housing—who had fought for something, rights that the United States had largely denied them when they returned home. Anne had mentioned that when she was growing up, living in the housing projects was an honor, as they housed some of the neighborhood's middle-class families. In its current state, the public housing where Dametria lived was often lifted up as an example of what happens when self-reliance and pride are absent.

Daron discussed racism as a structure in which people get caught up, recognizing the challenges that Black folks might experience. At the same time, he relied on a nostalgic past to frame responsibility. Rather than suggesting adjustments to or abolishment of racist structures that disproportionately affect Black people, Daron suggested that a lack of self-reliance on a community level caused the community to be in a place of disadvantage or suffering:

> If you go into the housing authorities, you go two generations back. You try to get away from racism, but they're caught up in the system, and it's generational. Some people get out; most people get out, quite frankly, but some don't. That's where we are now. We've lost those basic traditions. More importantly, we've forgotten why. Now we suffer. Our health suffers. Our economic system suffers. We still don't trust each other. I've experienced enough disloyalty and corruption in my own community, I understand completely now why we are so divided. We have no unified system. Every time we get close to unity, somebody from within does something so diabolical to interrupt and undermine it. It separates us again. What I saw was that the ones that survived . . . the ones that was afforded opportunities as a result of our parents, and my grandparents' struggle in the civil rights movement . . . forgot what their responsibilities were. They really believed that at the time, that they were entitled to the proceeds and the profits, and they're supposed to be comfortable. That's the opposite of what DuBois wrote about. That's the opposite of what Carver wrote about, and King.

Initially, Daron implicitly identified systematic failures by talking about how families get caught up. However, his quick pivot toward internal distrust and division, disconnect from a shared vision, and lack of collective struggle placed responsibility for suffering squarely at the community's feet. By calling forth a longer legacy of struggle for civil rights, Daron offered a sentiment similar to those voiced by Anne and Cliff, both of whom suggest that not only are younger generations disconnected from a legacy of civil rights but also that they did not care as much as previous generations, and that this lack of care undid some of the work that previous generations had fought for.

For some, this was a failure in terms of what older generations taught their children to value. One participant recounted:

> I asked [an elder]. What he said was, "We wanted our kids to go to college. We couldn't go. We couldn't get government jobs, so we wanted better for our young people, and that's where we went wrong." I said, "What do you mean?" He said, "Some of them, well, being an employee is really not a better situation, unless you're an employee of your family's business. We make sure our children have an education, but most of them got an education, and they're taking it and working for other people, in other communities, and none of that has really trickled back to our community, to build up our own businesses."

As Keeanga-Yamahtta Taylor notes, how Black people in the United States engage inequities is varied and complicated, sometimes resulting in internalizing responsibility for systematic failures, because there is so much at stake.[17] Participants never framed their assertions as taking responsibility for the state's and corporations' failures, however. Instead, the belief in and reproduction of narratives of self-reliance functioned as both a reflection of embodied understanding of how systemic failures were normative and consistent and as an example of how it is possible that inequalities reproduce themselves. When the state fails, who is there to fill in the gaps? As the narratives presented in this chapter suggest, nostalgic imaginaries do not forgive or erase inequities, but they are strategies through which residents sought to reclaim power.

Conclusion

The ways residents remembered, imagined, and engaged the past were important, because they measured (or critiqued) food access and consumption in the present based on the nostalgic food imaginaries they created. The emptiness that Anne alluded to when she gestured to the field across from her home was spatial, metaphorical, and deeply personal, not only in her own experience but also in that of others, as residents wove together spatial, communal, and individual food histories to create a version of the past that had implications for how they moved back and forth between understanding structural constraints and internalizing responsibility for the lack of community cohesiveness and food retail.

As is often the case with nostalgia, people remember the good or best parts of their past experience. It is particularly strong when people are navigating inequalities on a daily basis and have experienced or have constructed narratives of times when those inequalities did not exist. In this case, the unequal food landscape was this backdrop, and residents compared the worst of the contemporary to the best of the past. This is not uncommon in African American stories or oral histories, as the conditions of racism and white supremacy sometimes result in people locating the most productive, the best, or the strongest racial solidarity and self-determination elsewhere.[18] Because of this, some researchers critique the use of oral history and historical memory because they are not always logical in their adherence to fact. However, historical memory and oral histories offer much more than a mechanism for verifying the where, when, or how of events or places related to Black experiences. These stories of the past reveal much about the collective process of making sense of emptiness or lack of adequate food access. Or, as Alessandro Portellie argues, "The importance of oral testimony may lie not in its adherence to fact, but rather in its departure from it, as imagination, symbolism, and desire emerge."[19] This collective historical memory and longing for the past are starting points for examining how the past functions in the social commentary about food access provided by residents. Connections among Blackness, identity, and nostalgia demonstrate how imagined pasts provide important data for understanding the social change people would like to see or aspects of community life that they believe no longer exist.

CHAPTER FOUR

He's Had That Store for Years

The Historical and Symbolic Value of Community Market

Meeting Mr. Jones

I met Mr. Jones, the second-generation owner of Community Market, in the fall of 2012. I had interviewed Karen, a woman in her late thirties who left Deanwood for college only to return in the 1990s, and she mentioned him. Karen, who took a special interest in my project because she too studied anthropology, asked, "Have you met Mr. Jones yet?" When I said no, she laughed and said, "Well you definitely have to meet Mr. Jones. He's a trip. Tell him I sent you." Following Karen's recommendation, I set out to meet Mr. Jones. One afternoon, I pulled up next to Community Market, a store I had passed while exploring the neighborhood.

I walked into the store and approached a stout, dark-skinned man wearing a maroon apron and a diamond stud in one ear. He was sweeping. "Are you Mr. Jones?" I asked. There was a long pause between my question and his answer, during which he continued to sweep. When he stopped sweeping, he looked me in the eye and said, "No." I extended my hand for a handshake, introduced myself, and told him who sent me and that I was looking for Mr. Jones because I was studying food in the neighborhood. His demeanor softened into hearty laughs. His response—"Tell that girl I'm gonna get her!"—revealed to me that he was, in fact, the person I was looking to meet.

Mr. Jones welcomed me in as he put the broom aside and sat in a black swivel chair. I learned early that my time with Mr. Jones would require little talking from me. He was ready and willing to share his experiences and opinions. On the first day we met, he propped his folded arms across his stomach and talked for an hour. I scanned the store while I listened. The size of a typical "corner store," Community Market was neatly organized: stacked canned goods lined the shelves on one wall. Center shelves held essentials such as toilet paper and laundry detergent as well as sodas, juices, and water. The refrigerator units were on the wall opposite the canned goods. The few fruits and vegetables—which were supplied as part of a collaboration with a local organization aimed at increasing the availability of fruits and vegetables in low food access areas—were nestled in the back corner. Candies and gum made their home behind the register.

FIGURE 6 Fruits and vegetables at Community Market. Photo by the author.

Mr. Jones talked and talked as I furiously captured sound bites on the notes app on my cell phone. "This is a war," he said. "It's hard to fight. When kids walk out the door with money in their pockets, they can buy whatever they want." He focused on children and youth during that first conversation, leaving me to wonder more about his role in the neighborhood as both a community member and a grocer.

In the contemporary food landscape, Community Market seemed like *just* a store one block from another corner store. On the outside, nothing distinguished them. It sat on a corner lot facing a busy thoroughfare, surrounded by a few churches, a barbershop, and a vacant soul food restaurant that had been closed for years. Like others in the area, the building was small, displaying the store's name in bright red letters and having bars on the windows. There was a small sign, the size of a standard sheet of printer paper, warning patrons that they must be "properly dressed" to enter the store. Early in my fieldwork, however, it became clear that Community Market had historical significance. Community Market, which was originally a grocery store and a gas station, opened on a corner lot in 1944. Despite the fact that grocery retail was consistently and rapidly moving toward large chains and supermarkets, Mr. Jones's father opened Community Market. Although stores like Safeway and Giant were gaining traction, Black-owned busi-nesses remained a mainstay in segregated neighborhoods, as they were central to continuity in economic and social life.[1] With Jim Crow laws and continued political and economic discrimination that shaped race relations in the District,[2] Community Market represented a distinctive component of grocery shopping, food consumption, and everyday life. Black-and-white photos show the original brick building advertising its goods in uppercase white letters: GROCERIES, VEGETABLES, FRUIT, FISH, POULTRY. Inside, shelves were carefully stocked with canned goods, baking needs, and sodas, while the deli in the back offered selected meats.[3] As explored in this chapter, entrepreneurship, one of the primary avenues through which Black residents created stable communities at the beginning of the twentieth century, remained an avenue through which residents believed commu-nity stability was possible.

As noted in chapter 2, research participants included various stores in their everyday food shopping, but Community Market was not regularly one of them. Although I spent many hours observing the store, its owner, and its patrons, none of my research participants shopped there regularly. There were many opportunities for me to potentially interview patrons who came into the store, but I consciously chose not to seek interviews with the store patrons for several reasons. First, the store owner, Mr. Jones, readily agreed to allow me to sit in his store whenever I wanted. During the first three months of hanging out in the store, I noticed that—outside of after school-rushes when the local middle and high school students came in—clientele was scarce. I was hyperaware of this, and did not want to potentially insert myself in disruptive ways.

Second, I used the snowball method to gain participants in this study. As such, I followed the connections; I followed the friendships, relationships, and recommendations. Though I asked if he thought there was anyone I should interview, Mr. Jones never offered any of his patrons as potential interviewees. Finally, and perhaps most important in the context of this chapter, I wanted to see how or if the meaning of this store would emerge organically from any of my participants. This, I thought, would reveal some interesting nuances in how this store was read and experienced by Dean-wood residents. Among my participants, seven of them spoke meaningfully about Community Market and Mr. Jones. Those seven participants varied in age and gender, but they all shared one commonality: they identified as middle class.

This presented a conundrum: How is it that those seven participants spoke so passionately about the store and cited its significance to the neighborhood but at the same time did not economically support it by shopping there regularly? Anne, Irma, Janice, Koti, and Daron, for example, all knew Mr. Jones personally, and claimed Community Market to be indispensable not simply for the food it provided but also for the space it claimed as a Black-owned business. It was not important, however, because it figured prominently in their food geographies. Instead, they each discussed the store in the context of the neighborhood's history, change, and community. Chapter 3 discussed how the absence and memory of retail and community structures of the past categorized how people constructed and operationalized nostalgic imaginaries; this chapter explores the sometimes contradictory meanings of a store around which the imaginaries were no less palpable but instead were built around possibilities rather than absence. As a physical representation of what is possible for Black-owned food retail, residents' stake in Community Market was high. It represented the very imagined community that many discussed in chapter 3: a thriving Black enclave with diverse food retail and resident-supported Black-owned businesses. The store was a symbolic representation of self-reliance and communal responsibility. Its precarious future was a metaphor for how many felt about the future of the neighborhood.

In this chapter, Community Market serves as the departure point for examining how participants made meaning of this store's historical, social, and racial significance by distinguishing it from being "just another corner store." Participants wove a web of significance that included race, history, and changes in the food system by positioning Community Market as a physical and historical representation of the type of community they wanted to see. Throughout this chapter, I explore how Community Market held multiple meanings within several liminal spaces: the space between corner store and neighborhood grocery; between past, present, and future; and between staying "as is" or changing for the evolving demographics that Ward 7 residents anticipated as a result of gentrification.

The Grocer Speaks

When I visited the store during the week, I would often gaze on a familiar scene: Mr. Jones—sometimes wearing his maroon apron, sometimes not—sitting in a chair behind the counter, watching people walk past the window of his store. More often than not, he wore dark-tinted sunglasses, even when there was no sun. "Hey baby!" he would call out after he heard the bells clink on the door to signal that someone was entering and subsequently recognize me. "Hey! You know I had to come see my favorite person," I would say occasionally. This pleased him immensely, as it gave him great satisfaction that I chose his store as a place to observe during my fieldwork and that long after I completed formal research, I still continued to come to the store to check on him.

Customers trickled in slowly throughout the day. It was easy for me to tell who was familiar with the store and Mr. Jones and who was not. Sometimes, people came in looking for beer. They would walk around, checking every refrigerator in the small store. Mr. Jones knew what they were looking for, but he waited until they asked.

"Got any Coors Light?"

"Nah, I don't sell that here."

With that, the would-be customer would leave unceremoniously. Mr. Jones looked forward to those he knew, speaking their names, asking about their families. Sometimes elderly men would come in and talk for a while. Whenever I was around for this, Mr. Jones put on a great show, pulling the men into conversation about relationships, which often focused on giving gendered, unsolicited dating and marriage advice to me that was rooted in respectability politics:

MR. JONES: [*Addressing a customer*] Even with her, I say make sure
    that man's got a job.
REESE: Yeah, he tells me all the time. He tells me all the time.
CUSTOMER: That's right.
MR. JONES: Make sure they got a job.
CUSTOMER: If you date them, it can go both ways.
MR. JONES: Yeah it goes both ways.
CUSTOMER: They need to make sure you gotta job too.
MR. JONES: Yeah. Ain't going to be no sitting home. Not with only
    one check, it ain't happening.

The quiet, lazy tenor of the day would change around 3 P.M. when students trickled in from local schools. They entered Community Market in hordes. The store down the street demanded that students only enter two or three at a time. Mr. Jones did not have the same demand, but he did require them to make a single-file line when making their purchases. No loitering outside his door. No cursing. Tone down the horseplay and loud talking. On one occasion, in a span of about ten minutes, fifteen kids had entered the store. Then there was a lull. Around 4:29, a louder, rowdier, and seemingly older crew came to the store. The loudest, cussing ones stayed outside, but it was not long before Mr. Jones shooed them away from his storefront. They fussed, but they crossed the street to wait for their friends. For the after-school crew, Community Market was a go-to spot for quick snacks. Some called Mr. Jones by name. He asked several about their families.

"How you doing, Mr. Jones?" one young man wearing an ROTC polo shirt asked as he grabbed a ninety-nine-cent bag of chips. Mr. Jones nodded in his direction and asked how his day was. Another boy, younger—probably in middle school—asked, "What can I do with fifty cents?" as he grabbed a brownie off the shelf. Two girls walked up to the register. One, holding a bag of Doritos and a kiwi-strawberry drink, turned to her friend and said, "My favorites." "Hmmmph. Makes you fat," Mr. Jones responded. Both girls giggled, paid, and exited the store. If the two girls wanted other options within a half a mile, they could have gone to one of the two corner stores that sold most of the same goods as Mr. Jones or walked further to the McDonald's. Aside from those, there were no other options. Corner stores, regardless of what students choose to buy, function as important sites for youth's autonomy—a third space between home and school in which they can make their own choices about what they consume.[4] Ironically, this choice is what Mr. Jones critiqued, but the kids chose to come to this store anyway. Elizabeth Chin notes that for youth in urban neighborhoods with low food access, stores like Community Market are not only places where they consume; they are also safe spaces where they are loved, valued, and not assumed to be deviants before they walk in the door.[5]

Mr. Jones treated the students with respect, even when setting firm boundaries. However, he also had strong critiques of youth broadly, displaying his authority as both an elder and a business owner who worked in the food industry. One day, with feet propped up and arms folded, he said, "Fast food and candy are teaching us to eat unhealthy." He continued, "We don't know how to eat celery or cabbage or brown rice anymore. They don't want it. They want what tastes good." By "we" he meant African Americans, tying himself and me together based on our shared racial identity. By "they" he meant African American children, signifying a generational shift in eating—one different from eating "whatever was put on his plate," because in his family, children did not regularly have a say in what they would eat. From Mr. Jones's point of view, he looked out for the kids, as he saw them from an "it takes a village to raise a child" perspective. This, coupled with his critiques of sugar, fast food, and video games, as well as his belief that the number of food choices kids have today is bad for their health, informed his decision to limit the sale of candy to kids. Mr. Jones used his position as the store owner and an elder to set boundaries and limits on what could be purchased in his store. Good health and eating nutritious food are largely attributed to individual choice and responsibility. My participants were no different in their expectations that, regardless of inequalities, it was their responsibility to make sure they and their children consumed healthy foods. Mr. Jones's decisions regarding his store begged the question, Who is responsible for healthy eating? In some ways, Mr. Jones embodied some responsibility for healthy consumption, and despite these limits, students continued to patronize the store, demonstrating its significance in their after-school food geographies.

Saturdays took on a different tone. They were convenient days for elders to shop at Community Market. One Saturday, I went to visit Mr. Jones at Community Market. While there, I watched his son do something that is not usually associated with "corner stores": he retrieved and packed up items for two elderly women who came to the store. The first woman pulled up alongside the store. From the driver's seat, she leaned over and handed Mr. Jones's son a list and some bags, and waited for him to do the shopping. He took the list and walked around the store quietly gathering her groceries as Mr. Jones and I continued to talk. After he collected everything, he took the bags back to the car, where she inspected them. One of the items was not correct, so he took it, exchanged it, and brought out the item she desired. She paid in cash, and he took her change back to her car. The woman drove away.

A second woman, who walked to the store using a cane, came in. She did not have a list, but it was obvious she was familiar with Mr. Jones's son, because she called out the items she wanted, and he retrieved them for her while she chatted with Mr. Jones and me about traveling, her daughter, and a community member I did not know. Including me in the conversation, Mr. Jones said, "She brought me this back from South Africa," as he showed her the necklace I brought for him during a traveling stint. "Oh that's nice!" she exclaimed and then began to tell us about her daughter, who did a lot of international traveling. Mr. Jones's son rang up her items, she paid, and she stayed to talk more while waiting for the bus that would stop about a half block away.

These interactions, though basically about purchasing food, were nestled within the larger neighborhood food landscape in which residents had varying goals and strategies around purchasing food. Michel de Certeau, Luce Giard, and Pierre Mayol positioned neighborhood grocers as central, public spaces of significance in neighborhoods:

It is at the grocer's that the neighborhood awareness is sharpened much more so than on the sidewalk or on the stairs. Why? Because buying is a public action that binds, not only by the price it costs, but because one is seen by others in the midst of choosing what will become a meal. One thus reveals something about oneself, about one's secret; this creates permanent availability for speech that, starting from the example of a comment on the quality of various products, takes off from the foundation on which it began rolling in order to rise up into a more general discourse on neighborhood events . . . *The grocer is where the neighborhood speaks.*[6]

If the *grocer* is where the neighborhood speaks, then Community Market had several things to say through the store itself and its owner. Many of the people who visited Community Market went there for many of the reasons I looked forward to going: the friendly banter, the feeling of almost stepping back in time, the feeling that you were going to visit someone who was not just trying to sell you something but someone who knew you and knew what was happening in the neighborhood.

Research participants positioned Mr. Jones as a moral authority in the neighborhood, one who had the best interests of the community—specifically the neighborhood kids—at heart. Koti highlighted how Community Market was distinct from other stores by pointing out the ways Mr. Jones exercises a particular type of moral authority within his store: "Except for the Safeway, there are pretty much just corner stores. Mr. Jones's store [falls] somewhere in between corner-ish, but still has more. At least he refuses to do certain things, like sell lottery tickets. He's like, 'I don't give a damn what people think about me not doing certain things.'" Talking about Mr. Jones's decision not to sell candy to his children, Daron explained:

> In his store, he sees young people who come in and buy a whole lot of candy. "I'm not selling you that." I'm like, this is the kind of thing that sometimes young folks don't respect, but they don't understand. All money's not good money to him. He's not going to take your money to your detriment. He's told me that a million times. I had an office right over there, and my mother had an office upstairs for two years. My kids would go downstairs. At first, I was like, "No," because I know they wanted to buy candy. They come back, and I'm like, "What's wrong?" "Mr. Jones made us get this." I was laughing.

Both participants drew from ideals of community that reflected their knowledge of the history of the neighborhood and a belief that shared responsibility was an important part of building community. This also gives some insights into the type of community they wanted to live in: one in which even business owners took responsibility for the kids in the neighborhood. This was not unlike Mr. Harris and Ms. Johnson, discussed in detail in chapter 5, who desired to build parents' trust and participation as their children were involved in the community garden. Though their social worlds did not collide, Mr. Harris, Ms. Johnson, and Daron all shared a vision of community that focused on creating safe environments in which children would be cared for and looked after by other community members. Daron pointed out, "All money's not good money to him," which illustrates a particular type of business ethic that was not only about consumer capitalism but was also reflective of a desire to invest in the health of the community.

This not only says something about Mr. Jones and Community Market; it also gives us more insight into Daron and Koti. Both participants called attention to Mr. Jones limiting the sale of candy and abstaining from selling lottery tickets, which are both associated with corner stores and small markets in low-income "food deserts." Their pointing out these aspects of his business and community practice suggests that they wanted to ensure that I knew that they did not see the store as "just another corner store." Indeed, it lends itself to thinking about Community Market as distinct; but it also lends itself to deeper understanding of who Daron, Janice, and Koti thought themselves to be: community-oriented, socially conscious citizens who wanted to support a Black-owned business. Thus, the businesses they vouched for reflected those values.

If the grocery is where the neighborhood speaks, Community Market held multiple meanings: not *just* a corner store, a symbolic representation of the moral authority Black-owned businesses can have, and the contradictions of self-reliance. Community Market survived the transition from residents depending on small, neighborhood groceries to residents primarily depending on large supermarkets to meet their food needs. This transition affected not only Mr. Jones's clientele but also the meaning and practices of the store. What started out as a general store, serving the neighborhood alongside other neighborhood grocers, transitioned to being read as a "corner store" as neighborhood grocers and markets lost their significance and meaning as generations changed.

This larger transition has political and racialized significance. Since at least the 1970s, small grocery stores in the form of corner stores have re-emerged in urban areas, but they have been understood within a racialized frame. Seneca Vaught notes that the term "corner store" is racially coded, as they occupy space in some of the Blackest and most economically deprived urban areas,[7] paradoxically demonized for contributing to the so-called obesity epidemic while at the same time being some of the most accessible places for residents in food-insecure neighborhoods. Although some residents and youth supported Community Market specifically, the general vibe around corner stores was not positive. When asked about how the neighborhood food system had changed in other ways besides supermarket closures, one resident responded:

> The mom and pop stores are a problem. You got more fast-food places around here than you do healthy food options. You got Denny's. You got every mom and pop corner store. One of the things that's kind of funny is that, and somebody pointed it out, you got something called the grocery store [in their name], but they don't have any fresh produce in it. They got a few items like canned goods, all that kind of stuff. That's what constitutes a grocery store. It's just sad. Also, there's a ton of stores over here, too. I know right down there, Marvin Gaye. You been down to Marvin Gaye Park? [*I mumble in the affirmative.*] Okay. Those kids [coming from school], all of them pass corner stores on the way to school. You know these kids are going by these corner stores when they first come to school in the morning. So most of the time they get a soda or some flaming hot Doritos, whatever like that. Then we watch them in class and for the first hour or two, they're flying off the chain. No control. Then at 12:00 you can't get them to do nothing. They crash. Whose fault is this? When we were kids, we had to carry lunches to school. You got stuff from home. You can eat the leftovers. You were eating lunch. You weren't eating junk. You might be able to buy cookies at school and stuff like that but that was a treat.

Though the question "Whose fault is this?" was rhetorical in this interview, in everyday life it carried weight, particularly in the context of the hypervisibility and awareness of non-Black store owners in a predominantly Black neighborhood. Politicians, residents, and researchers alike grapple with this dynamic. During a 2012 victory speech after winning a seat on the D.C. council, former mayor Marion Barry made the following remarks about Asian-owned businesses east of the Anacostia River: "We've got to do something about these Asians coming in, opening up businesses, those dirty shops . . . They ought to go. I'll just say that right now, you know. But we need African American businesspeople to be able to take their places, too."[8] Reactions to Barry's statements were mixed. Delegate Eleanor Holmes Norton commented that she was shocked and offended by the statements. Local business owners objected to the lack of specificity.[9] Barry initially defended his comments, grounding them in his desire for healthier, stable communities for African Americans east of the Anacostia River:

> I'm not doing anything except trying to have a renaissance of our community and get some respect. A number of these restaurants serve high-caloric food, bad food, et cetera, but the more important thing, they don't participate in the community. That's what I object to.
> I don't care who it is . . . Because that's reality. Who owns these little restaurants? Who owns them? You know, Asians . . . 90 percent of all the small restaurants in Ward 8, at least. We're spending our money there, and we demand respect. We demand they participate in community affairs. We demand they give jobs to Ward 8 people regardless of their cultural situation. That's as American as apple pie.[10]

Marion Barry's statements can be viewed as both problematic and illuminating. Singling out Asian-owned businesses as a monolithic group was offensive and echoed the same type of essentializing that Barry and others consistently fought against. His follow-up comments, however, also offer space for revealing how Asian-owned businesses were positioned vis-à-vis a decline in Black businesses, more joblessness, and increasing obesity rates. Barry's problematic statements highlighted a complexity associated with improving Black communities: the roles of race and businesses in community cohesion and stability. Statements about Asian-owned businesses in predominantly Black neighborhoods have been made by other politicians. Notably, Congressman Andrew Young made a statement similar to Barry's initial comments in 2006; he later recanted it and issued a public apology: "But you see those are the people who have been overcharging us—selling us stale bread, and bad meat and wilted vegetables. And they sold out and moved to Florida. I think they've ripped off our communities enough. First it was Jews, then it was Koreans and now it's Arabs, very few black people own these stores."[11] Thus, as the only Black-owned grocery retail in the neighborhood, Community Market operated within a space that was shaped by the politics of race and business ownership as well as residents' investment in and interpretation of Black-owned businesses in the neighborhood. Community Market was uniquely positioned historically and culturally. It operated somewhere between the neighborhood grocer model and the corner store model, but its meaning was largely constructed based on who was experiencing it. For Community Market, then, operating within the in-between space allowed for multiple interpretations in terms of how it was understood in relation to other stores in the neighborhood.

Within this context of racialized understandings of corner stores and ownership, research participants compared Community Market to other stores. Janice had gotten to know Mr. Jones fairly well by the time I interviewed her. As part of a community engagement project, she had profiled his and the few other Black-owned businesses in the neighborhood as a means of generating buzz about them that might translate into community support. When I asked her about how well-supported Community Market was, she responded:

> There's [another corner store] on Sheriff Road. And it's literally down the street from Mr. Jones's store. And people go there. Well, and that Asian store? Mr. Jones has, it's, you know, he's had that store for years. And it's like a grocery store. You know what I mean? It's literally a grocery store. And I was like this is a shame. But he doesn't care. He's like this is my father's business. He has his own customers that do come in and he has other businesses. So he's not hurt, you know what I mean? And people don't frequent. But I was just like this is sad. But people go [to the other stores] and play their lottery tickets. He used to sell lottery tickets in his store. So I think that's one of the big reasons why people don't go there. Because [why wouldn't they?] He sells some of the same stuff. He sells candy. He sells, you know, ice cream and all the junk food. But he also sells actual food. It's like a general store.

Neither Janice nor her husband shopped at Community Market, though she marked it as a grocery store that sold "actual" food. This presented a contradiction between theory and practice that pointed to the complexities of the value of neighborhood institutions within the context of everyday practices. She and her husband preferred stores in Virginia in order to get fresh fruits and vegetables for their children. Yet, Janice believed the store deserved support because of its historical significance in the neighborhood and because it is Black-owned. However, since she did not shop there, it begged the question, "actual food" for whom? She supported the idea and legacy of Community Market, which fell in line with her philosophies about more community engagement and support for local businesses. She continued:

Straight up, all these Asian, these Asian-owned little stores are the same. But I feel they don't get to know the community, they take the money from the community, and the community frequents their establishment. And it's just like there's no relationships being built. And it's just like I'm just here to take your money and some of them don't treat the people very nicely. They don't get to know the community they're in. They feel like I don't have to. I'm paying my taxes. I got my business and that's all I have to do. I'm like no. Do more outreach. I think here is like one store, if I'm not mistaken, that's kind of close to Marvin Gaye Park, that they donate to the baseball team. And if I'm not mistaken. I might be mistaken. But I think they donate to the baseball team. Or is that the McDonald's? I know the owner of the McDonald's does it too. But, you know, it's some that have been there so long that they do get to know people by just being there. And it depends on how you see a certain race or how you see a certain group of people. So I think it comes from lack of understanding, obviously. Ignorance. And I mean it doesn't help when you do have people coming in there and stealing. So I mean I don't know. I have mixed feelings about it because I'm like they have a right to be there. But at the same time I'm not all for the way they do their business a lot of times. And I'm definitely not all for them just coming in and not getting to know the community.

Like Janice, Daron also expressed a belief that Black-owned businesses were often overlooked, and also like Janice, he did not blame Asian-owned businesses. Instead, he believed that the scarcity of Black-owned businesses in Deanwood was a result of entrepreneurs not taking opportunities to develop food-related businesses, as well as consumers not choosing Black businesses: "Whose fault is that? It's not the Asians' fault that they took advantage of a food desert opportunity, and opened carryouts to sell soul food, which is ridiculous because it's horrible, too, by the way. It's really awful. The opportunity to create restaurants and businesses . . . we didn't do it. Now, we watch businesses come to our community that are African-based and they struggle, because we won't support them. We go right next to a Black-owned store that sells chicken. The same chicken wings; look at the Asians. Now, we have isolation." While Daron offered a critique of Black business owners for not creating businesses when they had an opportunity, Cliff countered with a different perspective: "They've been taught what to give you. They've been taught to work together as a team and we don't understand that. In their culture, they don't eat this mess. I know some. They don't eat this. They got us programmed." Cliff's words echo a constant theme among participants: a lack of community cohesion. This emphasis on lack of cohesion was framed within an understanding of a close-knit Deanwood of the past, which complicated constructions of community in the present.

Research highlights controversy and contention between Asian business owners and Black customers, including studies conducted in Washington, D.C.[12] While Chanhaeng Lee suggests that the strained relationships between Asian business owners and Black customers have been grossly exaggerated by the media, evidence from older Deanwood residents suggests that—at the very least—tension and economic competition (perceived and real) are important factors that shape how they view business in the neighborhood, including ownership.[13] Within this context, Community Market emerges as an icon, a symbol of the economic viability of Black-owned businesses. It embodies the self-reliance theme consistent throughout the neighborhood's history, which, for some, is synonymous with racial pride and progress.

Race, Ownership, and Moral Economy

On a micro level, Community Market operated within a moral economy tinged by racial solidarity, pride, and collectivism. Writing about food riots in eighteenth-century England, E. P. Thompson argued that histories of riots presume that the poor, often led by women, were spurred to respond to food shortages, and that the riots were prompted by hunger and lack that resulted from the rise in food prices as society moved more steadily toward a capitalist mode of production. Contesting this economic reductionism, Thompson argued that to understand the riots only as reactionary underestimated the significance of the political and social contexts within which they occurred: "It is of course true that riots were triggered off by soaring prices, by malpractices among dealers, or by hunger. But these grievances operated within a popular consensus as to what were legitimate and what were illegitimate practices in marketing, milling, baking, etc. This in turn was grounded upon a consistent traditional view of social norms and obligations, of the proper economic functions of several parties within the community, which, taken together, can be said to constitute the moral economy of the poor."[14] Put more simply, shortages and inequities were the conditions under which rioting occurred, but the community already had shared understandings about what food ought to cost and that everyone should have enough of it.

In anthropological literature, the concept of moral economies has re-emerged in recent years, although Palomera and Vetta contend that its recent applications often lose the centrality of class conflict and capital accumulation in favor of examining solidarity or alternative practices that emerge outside the market, or drop the production and distribution of resources from the analyses altogether.[15] For them, all economies are moral economies in the sense that they are guided by particular practices, values, and meanings—the mechanisms through which structural inequalities are reproduced.[16]

In the larger scope of capitalism, Black-owned businesses like Mr. Jones's are examples of why class analysis without racial analysis is incomplete. They are not separate from the larger ethos around capitalism that privileges individualism, competition, and meritocracy. Community Market was still a business. Mr. Jones was still concerned about profit, and the responses from residents indicated that they understood how competition shaped the field of food access. At the same time, however, analyses of capitalism without a racial analysis cannot adequately deal with the ways in which entrepreneurship for Black people needs to be historicized and situated within a context in which Black ownership is complicated by Black people's relationship to dispossession. Articulating what he calls the "black economy," Bobby Wilson argues that even after they gained freedom, the rates at which Black people were continually dispossessed of land and assets in the South created conditions in which a separate Black economy—one in which entrepreneurship was at the center—emerged in the segregated neighborhoods where Black people were clustered, creating a nation within a nation.[17] This was relatively short-lived, however, as Wilson continues to argue that, because capitalism requires an abundance of consumption to continue to reproduce itself, Black-owned businesses in segregated neighborhoods cannot compete with larger chains that have further reach within and beyond Black communities: "The relationship between capital and black economies amounted to something less than a complete separation. For the capitalist mode of production there is no outside. No places remain beyond the control of capital. Capital excludes nothing, not even the black consumer located in the most segregated parts of towns and cities."[18]

It was not that residents did not understand the extent to which grocery store and supermarket chains restricted the flow of capital within their neighborhood. It was also true that they shopped elsewhere anyway, demonstrating the extent to which practices like shopping for groceries can unintentionally maintain the status quo, which in this case meant that supermarkets reached Black consumers even if their stores were not in their neighborhood. What residents articulated, however, was that their hope was not solely in mainstream capitalism. In the micro moral economy in which Community Market operated, the values, practices, and meanings that shaped it were visible in both the critiques residents had of other stores and the value they placed on Community Market. This, on some level, was at odds with dominant capitalist thought. On the one hand, these residents discussed values that were antithetical to capitalism. On the other, these values were not employed in ways that translated into regular shopping or economic support. However, the desire to see Black-owned businesses, to wish them well, and to understand them as foundational to the vitality of communities was important to these residents and is not uncommon among Black Americans. "Is the business Black-owned?" is a question often asked among racially conscious Black people, and when offered a chance to support such businesses, celebration ensues. Black-owned businesses may not be an all-encompassing antidote to inequalities, but residents centering Community Market in their narratives reflected a belief that other values, such as collectivism and racial solidarity, were as valuable as food choice.

"Change Is Coming"

Though Community Market has historical and symbolic significance that has served it well, that should not be mistaken for an inherent ability to thrive through all economic or community changes. In Washington, D.C., gentrification is occurring at a rapid pace, and African American communities have suffered most. Deanwood, tucked away in the far northeast corner, was a "last frontier," meaning that gentrification gained momentum relatively late compared to other parts of the city, attracting young professionals and families. With an aging population with restricted mobility, homes lost to foreclosure or put up for sale after residents died or moved away, and some of the lowest real estate prices in the city, Deanwood and Mr. Jones's clientele were changing.

Mr. Jones admitted, though, that he has to make adjustments. When asked about how he decided what to stock in his store, he replied, "By what the customers want. I base it on who is coming in and what they're asking for." What customers wanted changed over the years, and his attempt to meet their needs was a balance between tradition and modernization. The deli section, for example, was not as popular as it was in its earlier days. With the convenience of packaged sandwich meats and cheeses along with packaged foods like Lunchables that widely appeal to children, deli cuts are not widely desired in Deanwood, but Mr. Jones kept the deli section running anyway. One thing customers asked for was more fruits and vegetables. Mr. Jones partnered with a local organization that supplied small grocers and corner stores with fruits and vegetables at a reduced cost to increase availability for customers in areas with low access. Mr. Jones reflected on these changes through the lens of a business owner:

MR. JONES: But they put up new structures all around us lately.

REESE: Yeah.

MR. JONES: They're all the same. If we [African Americans] don't buy it, somebody's going to buy it. But then a lot of business[es], like small stores, they go under, because the owners are dumber than the rich. I know a guy over there on H Street, he's got a restaurant down there.

REESE: Um-hm.

MR. JONES: His rent went up until his business closed. He's looking for a place right now. You know.

REESE: That's sad. But you own this building.

MR. JONES: Yeah.

REESE: Yeah. So you don't have to worry about that.

MR. JONES: I don't have to worry about that; but still. Change is coming.

REESE: Yeah.

Mr. Jones was acutely aware of the changes happening in his community. However, rather than theorizing about these changes from a structural violence perspective, which would call attention to the ways social, cultural, and economic structures were actively and systematically disenfranchising and displacing Deanwood residents and businesses, he placed the responsibility squarely on African Americans, even while acknowledging that small businesses were bearing the weight of these changes, demonstrating the contradictions and limits of individual responsibility. Mr. Jones's words show how he internalized the role of individual responsibility in larger sociopolitical shifts in the neighborhood. He continued:

MR. JONES: And then Black folks, sitting here don't see it coming. They just sitting around and do nothing. Stupid!

REESE: Hm.

MR. JONES: You know? You know, all of those [gas] stations out this way, owned by foreigners. When they all were owned by Blacks. Black people didn't pay attention. They killed it. All of the small, little restaurants. They're owned by foreigners now.

Mr. Jones offered both prophecy and critique, revealing the very real ways that he as a business owner could recognize the structural violence happening around him but at the same time ultimately resorting to offering strong words of reprimand for those who are most affected by it. "Change is coming" refers not only to changes in business ownership but also to changes in consumers. Mr. Jones framed African Americans as passive bystanders during these changes, contrary to what was explored in chapter 1. However, his commentary also highlights economic injustice that has—similar to earlier periods in D.C. history—disproportionately affected Black-owned businesses.

Mr. Jones referred to the H Street corridor when explaining changes that had occurred. The historically African American area, which was affected by the 1968 riots, had undergone intense gentrification since 2006 after nearly forty years of inconsistent investment. The few Black-owned food institutions in the area have struggled to stay open, because as the neighborhood demographics have changed from predominantly African American to predominantly white, some businesses have not been able to thrive.[19] While Mr. Jones suggested that "Black people didn't pay attention," the dynamic processes of neighborhood change, race, and the food system fueled unequal economic development and access in Washington, D.C.

Mr. Jones also tied neighborhood change to his store, his personal health and well-being, and the decline in customer patronage:

REESE: You worried about your store?
MR. JONES: Huh?
REESE: Are you worried about your store?
MR. JONES: I'm not doing nothing but paying the taxes [*laughs*].
REESE: [*Laughs*]
MR. JONES: Well, you know, you got to give it a concern, but, you know.
REESE: Yeah.
MR. JONES: How long will I be here? You know my age and my health, you know.
REESE: Yeah.
MR. JONES: But uh . . . you gotta play around with a lot of things, but, you know, you just gotta keep moving.
REESE: Yeah. Your store has been here so long, though.
MR. JONES: Yeah, but, let me tell you something. My job and my clients right now are spooks.
REESE: Huh?

MR. JONES: You know, people in this neighborhood, churches, we'll be our own downfall. We've taken everything from ourselves.

Similar to how he frames neighborhood change, seeing African Americans as the central figures responsible for stopping the changes, Mr. Jones suggests that even with the historical and symbolic significance of the store, patrons are fickle, and because of this, African American institutions in general would fail.

As he illustrated, Mr. Jones's store was in a precarious situation, despite the ways residents pointed to it as an important neighborhood institution. In his words and actions, Mr. Jones served as an example of what symbolic violence looked like at the intersection of community support, history, race, and shifting notions of neighborhood grocery retail. In Mr. Jones's case, he saw and experienced the birth and near death of this store. He saw how the community transitioned from primarily supporting neighborhood businesses to drifting to other neighborhoods and suburbs.

On the one hand, store patronage was important and had some bearing on what was happening. But on the other hand, a focus on store patrons revealed only part of the story. Socioeconomic status, competition with supermarkets, and the changing meaning and status of small grocers also contributed to the precarious position of Community Market. Mr. Jones, however, internalized a view of social and community responsibility based on holding African Americans accountable in ways that relied on self-reliance rhetoric that acknowledged structural changes in neighborhoods but gave little attention to how those structural changes influenced the decline of those stores.

Conclusion

Community Market held symbolic importance, even when residents did not choose to economically support the store on a regular basis. The store represented continuity, self-reliance, and communal responsibility. The lack of grocery stores in the neighborhood elevated the significance of this particular store, especially because of the dearth of Black-owned food retail in Deanwood in particular but also in urban centers more broadly. For elders and after-school students, Community Market figured into their practices of everyday life. For my research participants, Community Market existed at the nexus of preferences and the complexities of community support. Mr. Jones was an example of a business owner who prioritized relationships over profits—which was at least partially possible because he owned the building that housed the store. Yet, in the context of a changing city, it was unclear how long that would continue to pay off for Mr. Jones, as he considered renting or selling his store to someone else. For some, even the threat of Community Market closing made them pause. As Janice exclaimed, "He's had that store for years." The thought of it no longer existing or being owned by Mr. Jones was inconceivable. Community Market was a store through which my participants articulated why neighborhood institutions matter: the relationships that are built, the standards of care that are established, and an interest in community and well-being. However, participants' verbal support of Community Market contradicted their grocery shopping practices. This contradiction demonstrated the multiple ways people were nourished by this store. Community Market gave Deanwood residents space to connect in ways where their needs—physical, ideological, or interpersonal—could be met.

CHAPTER FIVE

We Will Not Perish; We Will Flourish
Community Gardening, Self-Reliance, and Refusal

A Garden Takes Root

The whole area was abuzz. Adults flowed in and out of the kitchen in the community center, huddled together having conversations in all the available spaces that did not obstruct the walkways. Others rotated between receiving health screenings provided by volunteers from the Student National Medical Association (SNMA) and standing off to the side as if to not fully participate in the activities. About a dozen children worked the garden, pulling weeds, planting new seeds, watering the soil. Others picked up trash and unused gardening materials. The garden itself was composed of three raised beds within a gated area and two other beds that were being constructed outside the gate. Mr. Harris, the primary contact for the garden, was off to the side, cleaning out what he called the "experimental bed," where he hoped to try his hand at plants he had not previously grown. At the heart of the activity was a makeshift dance floor, a grassy space that was taken up by adults from the community, children, and students from the SNMA. Our hips gyrated as the D.J. blasted:

Wobble baby, wobble baby, wobble baby, wobble, yeah
Wobble baby, wobble baby, wobble baby, wobble, yeah
Wobble baby, wobble baby, wobble baby, wobble, yeah
Wobble baby, wobble baby, wobble baby, wobble, yeah
Get in there, yeah, yeah
Get in there, yeah, yeah
Get in there, yeah, yeah
Get in there, yeah, yeah
Ay big girl, make 'em back it up, yeah, make 'em back it up
Ay big girl, make 'em back it up, yeah, make 'em back it up
Ay big girl, make 'em back it up, yeah, make 'em back it up
Ay big girl, make 'em back it up, yeah, make 'em back it up

This was a big event for the community and the garden. Green Space,[1] a local grassroots organization, provided gardening tools and cooking demonstrations throughout the year and the SNMA partnered with residents to

FIGURE 7 Residents and volunteers "wobble" together at the
Community Planting Day. Photo by the author.

host a Community Planting Day and Health Fair. In addition to planting,
the physicians-in-training checked blood pressures, screened for diabetes,
and distributed information about health conditions that disproportionately affect African Americans. The grassroots organization supplied the
D.J. and the food, and managed the volunteers who helped with the planting. Attendees ate, participated in screenings, danced, and planted until
sunset. The laughter, food, and good-hearted fellowship overshadowed negative stereotypes associated with public housing, if only for the moment.

I moved through the space taking photographs of people — some I knew
and some I introduced myself to for the first time — enjoying the freedom
that taking photos allowed me as a participant observer in that space. I was
happy to contribute in this way. Being the photographer was symbolic of
what this research was about: documenting and witnessing the nuances of
food consumption, production, and access in everyday life. I let the "expert"
in me take a backseat while I snapped photos, wobbled on the makeshift
dance floor, and met new people. That day, the crime rates and drug abuse,
and the reality that this housing project would be torn down, hovered in the
background as the event, focused on the garden, brought people together
for food, fellowship, and fun.

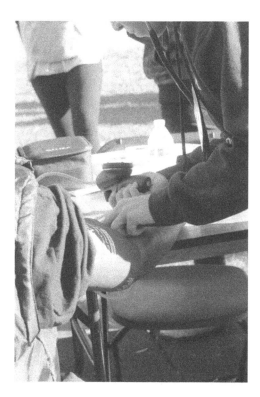

FIGURE 8 A volunteer from SNMA measuring a resident's blood pressure. Photo by the author.

The garden was a product of the local grassroots organization's desire to address food insecurity in predominantly Black neighborhoods and residents' desires to do something meaningful in their community. Joshua, who headed the agricultural component of the organization, was introduced to Ms. Johnson, who was the resident council president in 2011. As he learned about food sovereignty and food justice in D.C., starting a garden felt like a tangible solution that could be implemented immediately. "Starting a garden seemed like a great idea for bringing people together around something positive," he told me. Witnessing the Community Planting Day and Health Fair seemed to be evidence of the positivity he hoped to collectively cultivate.

For the gardeners, this was about more than growing food for the community. In 2008, the D.C. Office of Planning presented the Deanwood Strategic Plan, which was approved and later revised based on public comments. Largely drawing on Deanwood's history as a self-reliant community, the revitalization plan highlighted forty years of disinvestment while offering a vision that would restore Deanwood to the "eat, work, live, play, worship" community of its origins through public and private investments along the main thoroughfares to encourage "new mixed-use and mixed-income development in strategic locations that attracts jobs and creates a safe and pedestrian-friendly environment over a 10-year horizon."[2] The plan made no mention of the role of class and racial segregation in the forty years of disinvestment. Instead, it included removing residents from low-income housing units, tearing those units down, and rebuilding them as mixed-use and mixed-income buildings, even though failed attempts at this type of revitalization are well documented.[3] Residents who lived in public housing where this garden was planted awaited notice of what would happen to their homes and where they would be relocated. In the meantime, they created a community garden that reflected a commitment to continue living, despite whatever the future held.

As people were forcibly relocated and buildings were boarded up, this garden represented one of the ways its attendants engaged in acts of refusal that had implications not only for their food consumption but also for their attachments to the place they called home. The garden represented their determination and desire to remain where they had planted roots. In this chapter, I continue exploring the question, How do residents navigate and respond to the contemporary food landscape? Relatedly, what does it mean to engage these acts of refusal outside the immediate gaze of others, notably those in positions of power who had authority to make decisions such as redeveloping the housing community? Through an examination of this garden as a space where residents negotiated multiple needs and desires within the context of the failures of public housing and various—sometimes contradictory—framings of responsibility and community, this chapter explores how the dearth of local supermarkets shifted from being a societal problem to a community burden. This garden existed not only to address the tangible food needs of residents but also as a central physical space that attempted to address unemployment, youth development, and community pride.

The Makeshift Greenhouse

My first visit to the garden was in October 2013. Although I had been in touch with Mr. Harris for over a year, we had yet to meet in person. Prior to meeting, I drove around the community, taking in the identical dark-brown buildings that sat atop a hill. The dwellings had changed significantly since the 1940s, when families that included men who returned from war were the primary residents. They experienced a decline both aesthetically and financially, and the housing community was often cited as a central place for crime and drug activity. On that day, though, it was quiet, few people were in plain sight, and the only evidence of violence apparent to me was the boarded-up buildings that once housed families who had been relocated as part of the revitalization plan.

Mr. Harris met me at Ms. Johnson's office in the community center, which was a central meeting place. It housed social service agencies, a kitchen where cooking demonstrations were conducted weekly, and a small library that Ms. Johnson hoped to grow. As the president of the resident council, one of the perks of Ms. Johnson's position was having an office, which she shared with Mr. Harris so that he would have a place to work on administrative tasks related to the garden. The office reflected Ms. Johnson's belief that "it takes a village" to create community change. Posters of African American political and community leaders and photos from community events dotted the walls. An informational poster about Nannie Helen Burroughs, one of Deanwood's most well-known residents, hung on one wall. When I pointed it out, she said, "Yeah, see we have all the history and examples we need to be great. We just gotta do it." Alongside the poster was a rendering of the new mixed-income apartment building located less than a mile away. Some residents had been relocated there in advance of the projects' impending demolition. The juxtaposition of the two was jarring to me.

Mr. Harris was a tall, dreadlocked man—so tall that his head almost touched the low ceilings of his apartment. His kind eyes were set within dark skin, and he was missing his front teeth. The missing teeth did not keep him from smiling and laughing. As we walked toward his apartment, I observed that each building had an entryway that led to a stairwell. *This doesn't look any more inviting than a prison cell*, I thought. The buildings looked dark, neglected, and old. When we approached Mr. Harris's building, cinder blocks that had been painted a few times too many and poor lighting greeted us. Trash collected in the corner near Mr. Harris's doorway. He may have been embarrassed by it, because he commented on how the building was supposed to be cleaned but had not been. I felt like I had been there before. The buildings reminded me of the housing projects many of my middle school students in Atlanta lived in. Bowen Homes, which housed several thousand low-income and poor Atlanta residents, was torn down for mixed-used development, much as this one would be. Many of those who were relocated never returned, just as I assumed Mr. Harris and his neighbors would not. Thinking of that, I felt a wave of sadness and wondered what it is like to await forced relocation.

I did not have time to get lost in that thought, because when Mr. Harris opened the door, I had the answer, at least the answer for him. When we stepped inside his apartment, I exclaimed, "Wow!" Mr. Harris had turned his home into a greenhouse to incubate the plants that would eventually be moved to the garden for the next planting season. The gardeners had applied for funding for a greenhouse but did not receive it. Without the funding, Mr. Harris created an alternative solution in his home: a makeshift greenhouse. He cared for each plant—moving them around to get more light, watering them, repotting them. The plants spilled over into his kitchen. I wondered if he had any space to cook. I did not know where to start. I walked around his living room, touching the pots, admiring the art on the walls. When I asked questions, Mr. Harris eagerly answered:

REESE: So you got your lemon trees in here?
MR. HARRIS: Yeah.
REESE: I don't know what all these other plants are.
MR. HARRIS: Now this is an orange tree.
REESE: Okay.
MR. HARRIS: Now let me show you what they look like from the beginning [*pointing out a beginning plant*]. These are orange trees. This is how they start off. I used to have all the different stages. This is an orange tree I started from a seed.
REESE: So cool.
MR. HARRIS: Yeah.
REESE: So how long has it taken to grow this much?
MR. HARRIS: That's May. Since this May.
REESE: Ah, so nice. Now all this stuff you're gonna transfer outside in the spring?
MR. HARRIS: Exactly. Yeah. I'm using the light. Matter of fact, I'm getting a new lamp. Yeah. All that is . . . In fact, this is some type of new pepper. I put this in here [*a plastic container*].
REESE: Oh, I see.
MR. HARRIS: Yeah. Do you see the tag?
REESE: There's . . . yeah. Pepper. Orange peppers.

He explained every plant to me: where it came from, how he cared for it, how it behaved inside versus outside. Plants in recycled plastic juice containers, planters, and seeds and leaves in recycled Jello containers crowded the single window in the living room. He grew various peppers, tomatoes, lemon trees, orange trees, and a pine tree in his apartment. Mr. Harris showed me

FIGURE 9 Plants near the window in Mr. Harris's apartment. Photo by the author.

FIGURE 10 Beginnings of lemon and orange trees in Mr. Harris's apartment. Photo by the author.

a package labeled with words I did not understand. One of his neighbors was so excited about the garden that he ordered something called Sanchi Chaiyotsrichana from China. Neither he nor his neighbor knew what those seeds were. Neither did I. My Google search yielded no explanation.

Alongside the fruits and vegetables, a plant he called "the mother tongue," which is more commonly known as mother-in-law's tongue or snake plant, grew in various pots. He started those plants from a cutting he took from his grandmother—the person who taught him about gardening. He explained:

> MR. HARRIS: Oh yeah, the mother tongue. There's a story behind that. This is what happened. I don't know the correct name for it. Eventually I will find out, but my grandmother was put in a nursing home before she passed and so you know people just, "Oh we gotta get the stuff out of this house."
>
> REESE: Mm-hmm.
>
> MR. HARRIS: When nobody was looking, I got that plant out the trash. And I know it goes back several years because I was the one who had to go outside and bring it in the house when I was younger. So they go back. It goes back to . . .
>
> REESE: Back to your roots?
>
> MR. HARRIS: Back to my roots, yeah, because I'm the one that had to bring it in the house.

Ms. Johnson joined us as we moved from the apartment to the outdoor garden. The friendly back-and-forth banter between Ms. Johnson and Mr. Harris revealed that he deferred to her in matters of politics. Her questions about maintaining the garden showed that she respected his skills and decisions about the garden:

> MS. JOHNSON: So how is the Stevia plant doing?
>
> MR. HARRIS: Lost it.
>
> MS. JOHNSON: Oh! You're not going to do Stevia?
>
> MR. HARRIS: I transplanted it. Oh, it was looking beautiful and then I transplanted it.
>
> MS. JOHNSON: Awww. You lost it.
>
> MR. HARRIS: Yup. Didn't make it.
>
> MS. JOHNSON: You couldn't save the root . . . Can't you save sometimes parts of it and resurrect it?
>
> MR. HARRIS: I'm pretty sure.
>
> MS. JOHNSON: Uh-huh.

Ms. Johnson was the political pulse of the garden project. While Mr. Harris thought about the garden in terms of what it could do for the community, Ms. Johnson was more direct in discussing the opposition they faced from other residents when they planted the garden and developed programming around it: "Yeah. So, they were out there bad mouthing and you know, they didn't want to come at first, but since [the garden has] gone and [become] something and you know, activities come to it anytime, but oh God, it's some of them. 'I won't eat nothing out of it that. The soil is tainted, you know.' So, they were passing that word. I said 'Tainted? Tainted of what?' They said 'Blood.' You know, there used to be a lot of bloodshed right there." Together, Ms. Johnson and Mr. Harris had pride in the garden but also hope. The idea of the garden started within the community's resident council, and although some community members did not support it, it took root. In 2011, they were approached by a grassroots organization started by two Washington, D.C., natives. Together they developed a vision: use this garden as a way to teach about health, literacy, and eventually entrepreneurship. Three months after the community planting day, the organization was featured in a story on the local news. In it, one of the cofounders articulated their aim to partner with communities to address environmental and health concerns in food insecure areas rather than wait for additional businesses to come to the area. However, the partnership aspect of the organization and residents' work was obscured in the news segment. Rather than focusing on the collaborative effort between the organization and residents, the story centered on the organization. In the background of the video, Mr. Harris and others tended the gardens. The one resident who spoke highlighted the individual health benefits she had enjoyed as result of the garden: "This garden has helped me a lot with my health . . . I'm able to eat the kale in the morning in smoothies; at lunchtime the Swiss chard can be put on a sandwich of tofu and fruit." The community-building aspects other than individual health benefits were invisible in the news story. Food insecurity was the impetus through which the garden began. However, the garden became a space through which other issues affecting residents were explored and addressed. The garden was about much more than growing food.

Self-Reliance in the Projects: Responsibility and Community

I went to visit Mr. Harris and the garden not long after the health fair and planting day. We walked through the small, fenced-in courtyard that housed the three raised beds. From the courtyard, we looked out over a grassy hill

FIGURE 11 Bricks dumped at the foot of the hill where Mr. Harris wanted to plant watermelon and cantaloupe. Photo by the author.

where two additional beds had been added to grow kale and collard greens and where new fruit trees were planted. "Last year I had gotten all this flat," Mr. Harris said, pointing out to the grassy hill, which was in obvious need of both mowing and weeding. The previous year, there was some controversy around the fruit trees. Maintenance complained that mowing around the trees caused more work for them. However, when Mr. Harris volunteered to mow that section himself, he was denied the opportunity, presumably for liability reasons. The previous crop of fruit trees did not survive. "You know, it really looks nice with the [fruit] trees. You see them cuz they're sticking up in the air like that [*gesturing with his hands*] when the grass and weeds are low. The hill is hard to cut but we were able to get it down." Mr. Harris explained that once they got the grass down and the weeds gone, he hoped they could plant a watermelon and cantaloupe patch along the hillside, since there was very little chance they could plant another raised bed there. "Mmm-hmm, awesome," I said in agreement. "Yeah, it's a great view," Mr. Harris replied.

It was hard for me to see the great view Mr. Harris saw. I scanned the hill with its trees and tried to envision watermelons and cantaloupes. Instead of envisioning more fruit, I saw a pile of bricks. "What did they knock down over there?" I asked. "They knocked down something somewhere else that didn't work good," Mr. Harris responded. I gave him a confused look. "And then dumped their bricks over here? They just dumped them here?" I asked in sincere disbelief. Mr. Harris let out a laugh and said, "Yeah, that's how that works." Between this visit and the one two weeks prior, someone dumped a pile of bricks at the foot of the hill where the fruit trees and envisioned watermelons and cantaloupe would be. It was as if the garden, the housing units, or the people did not even exist, to which Mr. Harris responded, ". . . and that's what happens when you don't beautify your neighborhood before stuff like this happens."

Mr. Harris's words echoed the same sentiment that Dametria expressed when I interviewed her. Even though someone knowingly dumped those bricks in his community, Mr. Harris suggests that they would not have done it if community members would take it upon themselves to beautify the area. This resonated with what other Deanwood residents articulated about food access more broadly. Though the legality and morality of dumping bricks in an established community were questionable, Mr. Harris suggested that the community's lack of effort made them a target: "You know, because they're using anything to close this place. You know crime, you know. What they do is, they use stats . . . They will meet about this thing. 'But last year we did this. Oh it's gotten worse. It is 100, 200 percent worse than last year. Close it down' . . . So what we're trying to do is allow people not to impede their own progress with too much [laughs] misbehavior. At least start somewhere." Similarly, when I talked with Ms. Johnson about the property being closed, she used the garden as a symbol to explain her perspective on the community's closing:

REESE: How do you think the gardens are going to help this housing community? Because I know you know long-term the city has plans to shut all these down.
MS. JOHNSON: Oh you looked that up. [Laughs]
REESE: I've heard about it from several places, yes. [Nervous laughs]
MS. JOHNSON: Yeah, well that's why we whatever, you know because, you know personally, myself and then a lot of other people don't want it to come down.
REESE: Right.
MS. JOHNSON: We're not trying to let it come down. You see what I'm saying?
REESE: Mm-hmm.
MR. HARRIS: Alright now.

MS. JOHNSON: Then the garden and the trees and stuff are
representative of we will not perish—we're going to keep flourishing.
Flourishing.

"We're going to keep flourishing" is a powerful metaphor, particularly since many demographics signified that the community was *not* flourishing; and, relatedly, the city's plan was built on the idea that it was failing. However, gardening was an attempt to beautify while feeding. It was a method of active resistance in which residents exhibited agency in shaping some of the contours of their community. For these gardeners, flourishing was not simply about producing food. The desire and need to flourish were evident in all their programming.

In that vein, the garden flourished primarily outside the gaze of the larger food justice movement in D.C. and public officials. Dametria, for example, believed that the garden was not getting the recognition it deserved. Although she voiced concerns about the participation of community members and argued that the lack of resources is in part the community's fault, Dametria was hopeful about the garden. She believed it countered apathy. Dametria saw the garden as a success in the community and encouraged her two youngest children to participate regularly. As something they could be proud of, the garden could be shown off to others. Yet, this is where Dametria understood that even though they believed the work to be good and worthy of merit, others did not. Specifically, she spoke of this in the context of First Lady Michelle Obama, who, through her campaign to fight childhood obesity, has championed community gardens, healthy eating, and exercise.

It would be helpful if we can get like Michelle Obama to come out here and to do something in our neighborhood, because you don't find the President and the First Lady to come out in these types of areas. They don't even come in projects and it's sad. They go in high-quality neighborhoods and help out, but we're the ones that are really like low income and public housing . . . if we can get the news people out here one day when we're having a little green program out here, maybe we get some attention like "okay, we see [they are] trying to make a difference in their neighborhood. Maybe we can sponsor them or help them to get funding."

Dametria's narrative points to several interlocking processes. First, she offered a critique of President and First Lady Obama's decisions regarding the areas they visit. By leaving out the projects, the Obamas excluded a population that, as Dametria alludes to, is the real population that they should be trying to reach. Indeed, childhood obesity and low food accessibility affect low-income and poor populations more than others. As such, this community's attempt to create a solution that potentially addresses both aligned with Michelle Obama's campaign; yet, with little visibility, it is as if it did not exist. This invisibility reinforced the notion that the community's problems were created by them and must be solved by them, though the problems were much bigger than the sum of their individual actions.

Navigating Needs: A Balm in the Projects

On one level, the garden was created for the same purposes as many other contemporary community gardens in urban neighborhoods: to address the lack of fresh fruits and vegetables within reasonable reach of residents who need them and to educate residents about food production and healthy eating. On other levels, however, the garden became a metaphorical representation and critique of this model. With goals to use the garden to teach entrepreneurship, parental involvement, and management strategies, and to use it to help shift toward communal ownership to hopefully alleviate stealing, those in leadership also understood that this garden could not address the food-related needs of community members without addressing other needs.

One of the ways the garden committee thought about sustainability was by considering how to sustain the community as a whole, and not simply the garden. Maintaining a healthy, thriving garden symbolically represented the healthy, thriving community they wished to see. In an analysis of ten community gardens in Baltimore neighborhoods of varying socioeconomic status, Melissa N. Poulsen et al. reported that those involved in community gardening considered their work as part of constructing an "urban oasis" that yielded benefits not only for the individual but also for their communities.[4] In a similar way, the gardeners at this housing project explicitly rejected notions of individualism through envisioning and planning for opportunities for community members to thrive and grow. With no partitioned plots that were the responsibility of individual people, the garden's design encouraged this type of communalism. Though everyone was not involved in the upkeep, everyone was welcome to benefit from it, including financially. Instead of the conspicuous consumption model of community gardening, this particular garden was constructed and operated as a form of community survival.

FIGURE 12
Mr. Harris and
Reese examining a
raised bed. Photo by
Markeshia Ricks,
used courtesy of the
photographer.

One of the many problems that residents at the housing community faced was joblessness. Throughout my interviews, residents lamented that not only were there no jobs; there was very little hope for jobs. The garden committee planned to address the hopelessness concerning jobs by using the garden as a space to promote entrepreneurship. The rationale was that if community members had something to be proud of, if they had a space that they could use to promote their well-being through business ventures, it would contribute to changing the culture of the place. Though the garden beds were small, great care was taken to decorate the surrounding areas. Art created by kids adorned the black fence that gated the courtyard. Inside the community center were even more creations: water bottles and jugs that had been transformed into artwork with caulk and paint.

THE GARDEN, THEN, functioned as a place from which other ventures could grow:

MS. JOHNSON: You know what too? Like I say, like with that, we trying to get them to [do] entrepreneurship [through] photo shoots they can have in the garden. I'm serious about that. And then sell little postcards or something. Provide a variety.

DAMETRIA: Yeah, that's something. Good variety.

MS. JOHNSON: Sell the little postcards with this, you know.

DAMETRIA: Yeah. And it's just more of what you're already doing, which is taking all the plans and using them for something good.

MS. JOHNSON: Something. Yes indeed!

MS. JOHNSON: Yes, 'cause see, we had thought like about expansion so we had asked [the Housing Authority] for like, [*responding to my nodding*] yeah, he told you about it? A greenhouse right here on the property. Then the next part is entrepreneurship, all right, something, or if people wanna take pictures in front of [the garden], just like people take a drop cloth and charge, what, $10. You know what I'm saying?

MR. HARRIS: Mm-hmm.

MS. JOHNSON: Like down at the clubs and stuff.

MR. HARRIS: Oh yeah.

MS. JOHNSON: That can take place with that. Yeah! That's magnificent, a whole lot of stuff going on. Mm-hmm.

MR. HARRIS: You know, you have people, they're business people, but like I said, it's contraband business.

REESE: Hmm.

MR. HARRIS: And, and what happens over here is once a person gets in trouble with these charges, uh, it's, it's a dirty trick because they really X'd out of other things . . .

REESE: Hmm.

MR. HARRIS: So we wanna address some of that. We don't want them to be X'd out of anything.

A large part of the responsibility of the garden fell on Ms. Johnson and Mr. Harris. However, when it came to volunteers, they had a steady stream of kids of various ages wanting to participate. One afternoon I stopped by the garden to try to catch Mr. Harris, but he was not around. Joshua, one of the volunteers from the grassroots organization that supports the garden, was preparing to water the plants. The community planting day had occurred three weeks prior, and some of the plants were already sprouting. Three kids — two boys and one girl — clamored for both his attention and their opportunity to get a hold on the water hose. When they saw Joshua enter the courtyard, they left their posts at the nearby swing set to help. "Okay, I wanna do it," said Deshun, the oldest in the bunch. "You can do the beds on the hill. The beds on the outside," Joshua replied as he dragged the water hose from its place at the side of the community center. "Where's Mr. Harris?" I asked. "I stopped by to see what's up with him." Joshua continued dragging the hose and said, "I'm not sure," with the three kids in tow.

"No! That's mine! Not yours!" Deamber, the young girl, shouted at Deshun as she swatted his hands away from the hose. Joshua had promised her that she could water the three beds that held various greens and peppers in the courtyard. Joshua tried to keep Deshun focused while Deamber slowly watered her section. "Come on, let's go before it's too late." Deamber leisurely watered the plants, taunting the two boys, who were eager to get their hands on the hose. Malcolm, the youngest of the bunch, turned flips while waiting. I found myself catching my breath every time his feet floated over his head. "Good lord, that's scary to me," I said to him after he completed two flips in a row. I was afraid he was going to hit his head on the concrete. He sucked his teeth and laughed, "I know how to flip. I'm good at it," flipping right after.

"Okay. My turn!" Deshun grabbed the hose from Deamber, who slapped him as he ran to the garden beds on the side of the hill. He climbed over the gate, pulled the hose through, and began watering. Joshua tried to guide him. "You gotta get the water inside the bed." "Turn up the hose!" Deshun shouted. Malcolm wiggled his way through the gate and grabbed at the hose, causing Deshun to lose his balance, spraying us all with the water. "It's cold!" Deamber squealed. And it was cold. With temperatures barely hitting 50 degrees on that day, the ice-cold water, coupled with the chilly temperature, caused us all to shrink back. "Homie, you're not supposed to get wet. You're going to get in trouble," Joshua said to Malcolm. "You're wetting me!" Deamber screamed. Malcolm laughed, "She don't care if my clothes get wet. Just not my shoes." Joshua helped Deshun regain control of the hose to finish the outside beds. "Good job. Good job. Now we gotta water the fruit trees," he said. "My turn!" Malcolm grabbed the hose and began watering the trees while his two friends, Joshua, and I watched. "You might want to be behind him and not in front," Joshua warned me. I moved to stand behind the three of them, watching the watering process.

When Malcolm finished, we all entered the courtyard. Joshua and I walked around the fence while the three kids climbed over it. Joshua pulled the leaves on a plant I did not recognize and handed a piece to each of the kids to taste. It was fennel. The kids had not had fennel before, and each of them reacted dramatically; but that did not keep them from asking to taste other plants. As we sampled different plants, I asked the kids what they liked about hanging out in the garden, to which Deamber replied, "Because this garden in special. Especially when you get food. Without food, we would all starve."

Similar to other community garden projects in urban areas, this garden had a focus on children and youth. Children and youth are often situated as teachable, malleable, and as the hope for the future. Relatedly, the central focus on childhood obesity placed children at the center of what is considered a national crisis in obesity-related illnesses and deaths. First Lady Michelle Obama's Let's Move! campaign, for example, centered healthy eating and exercise as solutions to end childhood obesity by 2020. As such, the gardeners' decision to focus on children and youth does not differ from others', although their reasons for doing so might be different.

Mr. Harris and Ms. Johnson were both excited and encouraged by the participation of the youth, but their involvement presented challenges. A few weeks after watching the kids and Joshua water the plants, I met Mr. Harris at the garden to see its progress. "The children are really benefiting from this because they look forward to it. I see the same ones coming back and getting involved," he said. "Yes, when I came up with Joshua a few weeks ago, there were three kids who came up and helped him water everything," I replied. Mr. Harris nodded his head affirmatively. We continued to talked about the logistics of the garden and managing the youth who want to help:

> Every time I come up here I duck in quick [laughter] because I can't give them a full day. Sometimes I'm not going to do that much, and then I like to work with tools and then I'd be concerned with injuries . . . I don't want to keep them away from what they would really like to do, but I just want to wait until there's more adult supervision. The executive director is aware of this and is in love with what we're doing. She gave us the go-ahead to expand [the garden] when we was getting opposition.

Youth could learn skills, stay busy, and contribute to the well-being of the community. Overseeing and managing them was a challenge for Mr. Harris and Ms. Johnson. I observed the watering process with Joshua for about twenty minutes, and even during that time I could tell that managing just the three kids was a task. They were eager and helpful but also energetic and hard to keep focused.

Ms. Johnson's approach to understanding the kids and their parents was from a perspective that cultivating trust, talent, and responsibility within intergenerational relationships was a worthwhile effort:

> They learn responsibility. Every Saturday, you know, something new. I said, you're supposed to be doing something to help your community. Then, we noticed that the parents, like a lot of the parents, they were observing us. We're just people, but they were sending their kids up here [laughs]. We were the community babysitters. They were sending them all there. I mean we had told anybody to come, but I guess [the parents] said "Now, you all keep them for us." You know, it was so funny. But what was great about it is this, it's that the community trusts us with their kids. That meant a lot. They then got to know us and all the good things.

As the gardeners navigated the tangible food needs of the community, they had to consider other needs, which included childcare and trust: "We're trying to get more parents involved. We're working on that and that's going to work because they got excited about this at the beginning. Well that, and they're trying to get jobs and things like that. So we definitely looking for much more participation this year with the adults . . . we don't have a problem with the youth. They're ready to work. I just want them . . . I don't want their parents to think we're taking advantage of them working for nothing. We can't push . . . this is what they want to do." Although they experienced the tension between wanting kids to participate but not having enough adult supervision to accommodate large numbers, both Ms. Johnson and Mr. Harris understood that part of what made the garden successful was the parents' willingness to let their children participate. For Ms. Johnson in particular, the village paradigm within which she worked required a level of trust that eased boundaries between individual families and communities. In other words, the parents and their children needed to feel as though their movement was not restricted. Mr. Harris hoped that, by gaining the trust of the parents, more of them would get involved with the garden.

Conclusion

The garden reflected tensions inherent in working to meet people's food needs under spatial and economic constraints. The gardeners employed self-reliance not only to transform space but also to transform people. They were clear about the ways they were continually failed by the state: unrelenting unemployment, lack of youth and job training programs, and the dearth of supermarkets. Drawing inspiration from former resident Nannie Helen Burroughs and many other leaders who centered Black agency in the pursuit of healthier lives, the gardeners' hope was grounded in a belief that they could help themselves and that it was their responsibility to do so—even in the face of imminent relocation.

The question of the long-term effects of their work remains. The garden was a literal and symbolic spatial reflection of their commitment to building a healthy community. This commitment, however, was unmatched by the city. Month after month, families were slowly relocated to other housing in preparation for destruction and redevelopment. At the time of writing, the redevelopment process was stalled, but not before already disrupting the community. In addition, the garden itself did not radically redistribute wealth, decrease reliance on supermarkets, or, as Dametria aptly observed, bring any noteworthy attention to how the residents were trying to help themselves. In some ways, their work could possibly be deemed unsuccessful because of the limited reach and capacity of the garden, especially since gardening goals are typically framed in terms of capacity to transform the local food system. Even with these tensions, however, Ms. Johnson's metaphorical use of flourishing stands out as what makes this garden and the gardeners' efforts extraordinary. In their attempts to address the effects of structural inequalities, they affirmed and claimed their humanity for themselves despite the constant, state-sanctioned threat to Black life. Embedded in the various threats to Black life, however, was an optimistic love for community, a belief in a redemptive love that covered a multitude of sins—in this case the scars of systematic racism and disinvestment embedded in the spatial distribution of food.

Self-reliance is neither simply cultural nor simply spatial. Residents' understanding of self-reliance was grounded in historical and spatial contexts, addressing structural inequalities while building community, using the garden as the central site through which to work. In this context, "feeding the community" took on greater meanings than providing fruits and vegetables. "Feeding" meant youth development, visions for entrepreneurship, and potentials for strengthening relationships with parents and caregivers.

The gardeners were not only part of a larger food justice movement but also of a long-standing history of African Americans depending on self and community to address structural inequalities. As Steven Gregory and Sabiyha Prince note, African Americans have historically rallied around issues in their communities that they did not believe would or could be addressed through policymaking alone.[5] Marcus Hunter and Zandria Robinson illustrate particularly well how this has been treated in research, arguing that studies on urban Black America have always reflected an ongoing tension: Should the focus be on the structural constraints or on the ways in which people make lives in spite of enduring inequalities?[6] Yet, these gardens show that calling attention to the agency of residents dealing with food inequalities does not diminish the realities of structural constraints. On the contrary, by paying attention to this particular form of Black geographies, we are better equipped to understand what is culturally and materially important for Black urban residents. In this case, it was not enough to feed families with food from the garden. Instead, the gardeners' wished to feed more than bodies. They aimed to feed the soul a serving of hope with a side of self-reliance.

Conclusion
Black Lives and Black Food Futures

> There ain't no negotiations on freedom. I spent all my time knowing things instead of believing them. And that's the first step to being free. When you can see past all the things that you know and believe something better.
>
> —AISHA HINDS as Harriet Tubman in *Underground*

> Hope is a practice.
>
> —MARIAME KABA (@prisonculture)

Nuancing Access

Urban neighborhood food access varies widely, with low-income and predominantly Black neighborhoods often faring worse than their middle-class and predominantly white counterparts. Painting neighborhoods with broad strokes provides a macro-level view of resources but reveals very little about historical or contemporary on-the-ground processes. Though not the focus of this particular book, these processes are global, as struggles for land, power, and capital continually leave Black and Indigenous people as well as other people of color in precarious positions.[1] The focus on spatial contexts has contributed to a nuanced understanding of the disenfranchisement of low-income and predominantly Black neighborhoods but has also obscured the agency of residents themselves or, as Julie Guthman writes, "assumes that the environment simply acts on people, so that people are objects, not agents, in these environments."[2] Far less attention has been given to how residents navigate low food access to acquire the food they prefer or need or to how people create meaning in the process of doing so.

Neighborhood-level ethnographic research uncovers how residents navigate their food environments in ways that might not be visible in broader contexts, such as the city or region. The neighborhood functions as an intermediary space where macro-level processes, such as where resources are placed, can be connected to micro-level processes, such as how residents determine what to buy and where to buy it from. It is a space where daily exchanges are made,[3] where perceptions of the neighborhood and availability can be explicitly tied to space, family, and social networks, and where heterogeneity can be explored.[4]

When it comes to food and the people and institutions that provide it, there is an inherent tension between the past, the present, and everyday life. Seeing Black food geographies at the nexus of these—past, present, and everyday life—requires a construction of food access that expands beyond where people shop or what they choose to eat. It requires a commitment to seeing places as fluid rather than static, as the use of the term "food desert" suggests, and it requires a commitment to seeing the agency of the people and institutions in these neighborhoods. It is a commitment to listening beyond powerful narratives that frame worthy, deserving food consumers as those who eat the "right" way.[5] Sidney Mintz suggests that how power is applied changes society's food consumption habits.[6] The power to name, the power to define certain spaces, and the power to label a neighborhood void of value influence community members' and outsiders' perceptions of the place. The desire to bring good food to communities of color can be so myopic that it overshadows or ignores the multiple ways residents are navigating not only the physical space but also ideological spaces.[7]

Research on transnational food corporations and a failing food system has lured many critical food studies researchers to turn their attention either to the macro level or toward alternative food movements. There are good reasons for this: our food system fails us on many levels, and looking for alternatives or solutions provides some hope and also demonstrates how communities take control and dream the world anew. However, it is in the interest of the communities we serve and care about not to overlook supermarkets entirely, given the fact that the overwhelming majority of U.S. citizens depend on grocery stores to meet most of their food needs. To ignore them is antithetical to understanding the everyday food geographies of the masses. Relatedly, supermarkets do not operate in a vacuum, just as people do not. Thus, I have focused on them as just one of three sites featured in this book. They are important, but they are not all-encompassing.

Black Food Geographies examines both the macro-level structures that influence and shape local food systems, including grocery store access, and the ways that residents have sought alternatives. Some of those alternatives are material: stores and gardens. Others are more abstract: memories, nostalgia, hopes and dreams. In all cases, the lives, stories, struggles, and triumphs represented in this book are as much about the endurance of Black life as they are about precarity produced by white supremacist patriarchal capitalist structures that shape the contours of food access and the lives we lead.

The two—life and precarity—exist in tension; the people profiled in this book are constantly figuring out ways to navigate that tension and the spaces in between.

Though all the participants were navigating food inequities, they did not all have the same experiences or struggles. Consumption decisions as well as how participants discussed those decisions demonstrated a myriad of ways that food consumption is, as Pierre Bourdieu argued, a reflection of social relations as much as it is about feeding the body.[8] Each chapter shows this in different ways: through analyses of how the local Safeway is discussed in tandem with other shopping options; how residents discussed the importance of Community Market but did not choose to shop there regularly; and how residents discussed and critiqued themselves and their neighbors vis-à-vis history, nostalgia for the past, and investment in a meritocracy that required Black excellence, even when the state and corporations systematically failed Black people. Even with these class differences, the consistent theme of self-reliance reflected where and how residents placed their hope for a different spatial configuration of food and community relationships. The nostalgic imaginaries that circulated were embodied in different ways—discussions about Community Market and the community garden were the most salient—and reflect the importance of nostalgia beyond feelings or yearnings for the past. As Lorena Munoz argued, nostalgic imaginaries' power lies in the ways they draw entrepreneurs and consumers together and how they influence spatial practices.[9] The intimacy that is created is arguably at the heart of what many of the residents were looking for when they discussed community relations. A question that remains is how or if this power can (or should) be harnessed to transform local food systems.

Beyond Food: Black Lives and Precarity

Joao Vargas argues that Black liberation organizations and movements, even in their failures, provide blueprints for revolutionary change.[10] If organizations and movements provide blueprints, then the quiet refusals featured in *Black Food Geographies* offer micro-blueprints that unfold in everyday life. Intentionally, the lives and stories are not about organizations or movements but instead call attention to the ways individual residents make sense of and navigate the food system, make ways out of no way, and live lives that do not start or stop at the door of the supermarket. Knowing the hows and whys of accessing food within the context of people's real lives is important and strengthens the organizations and movements that seek to improve Black life. These micro-blueprints show how people are making lives, even when constrained.

One of the ways they do so is through the use of self-reliance as a framework for understanding lack, for filtering contemporary experiences through memory and nostalgia, and—as was particularly the case for the garden—for altering the landscape to meet their needs. And yet, there were limits to self-reliance. A few weeks before Mother's Day in 2015, I sat on the floor of my apartment. I had prepared all the things necessary for a night in of reading and writing: wine, a cheese plate, candles. At the tail-end of a lengthy project, I was setting the mood to flow with (and hopefully not against) the words on the page. In the spirit of procrastination, I checked my e-mail before writing. Seeing the name of a food justice comrade from D.C., I clicked on an e-mail. A eulogy stared back at me. I frantically googled his name, and sure enough I found a headline announcing that Caylon, the person who articulated *nothingness* so well in chapter 2, had been murdered in northeast D.C. in the middle of the night when many of us were sleeping. I reached out to another food justice colleague in D.C., who confirmed the news. It was true. Caylon left scores of people who loved him, including me.

I did not finish the cheese plate that night. I did not get any writing done. Instead, I thought about Caylon, his life and death, and what it meant to live in different levels and states of precarity. I, like others who knew and loved him, was grieving. In the minutes, hours, and days that followed, I grasped for tools and theories to help me process this. As an anthropologist, I was no stranger to the closeness one can feel with participants. But as someone who had spent nearly three years talking to people about food, inequalities, and their lives, I felt blindsided by this death that I did not expect.

The thing is, however, I may not have expected it, but everything I learned from community members about food access inequalities and their lives paved the way to understanding and theorizing Caylon's life and death at the intersections of multiple oppressions, constrained choices, and human agency. Grief happened to be the methodological tool that brought me to a place of connecting the dots, perhaps because in many ways Caylon's death felt personal. In "Theorizing a Black Feminist Self in Anthropology," Irma McClaurin argues that the field experiences of Black women scholars are often radically different from those of our white counterparts, and these differences have potential for producing rich theoretical interventions that are often dismissed under the guise of lacking "objectivity."[11] The autoethnographic approach to anthropology that McClaurin and others advocate for is essentially an approach that makes visible and embraces the fact that for some

Black feminist anthropologists, there is no hard and fast distinction between "us" as researchers and "them" as the community in which we serve.

This is not to paint a romanticized view of Black feminist anthropologists, especially those who identify as women, being wholly accepted or not experiencing challenges. In the field, my gendered self received many unwanted comments and advances. Perhaps naïvely, I had not anticipated being asked out on dates or approached by men who were interested in more than just my research project. I did not anticipate a parent asking me out in front of his daughter, insinuating that he would do the interview with me if I would agree to dinner. I did not anticipate a security guard at the recreation center saying "Maybe we can be more than friends" despite my assertions that I was in a committed, monogamous relationship at the time. I did not anticipate all the references to my body. I had to take a step back and really think about how I wanted to deal with such things in the field. Did I want to take a hardline approach? Did I want to dismiss the requests for dates or the references to my physical appearance? In the end, I treated each case individually. If I felt like I was being disrespected, I said that. If I thought someone truly wanted to just compliment me and move on, I accepted it and left it at that.

It is to say that despite or perhaps because of these challenges, the point of departure is often not the discipline itself but one's own body and one's own communities. Though D.C. was not my "home" community, it became one of the places I called home because of people like Caylon. Thus, his death was not just something that happened to him; it influenced/altered how I understood D.C. as home, D.C. as a violent space for people I love, and the very real tension of being "in the field but not of the field." Grief was instructive. In food studies, there is very little writing about caring for the communities we serve. The grief I felt and still feel was instructive for me in terms of how I would see myself as a researcher, yes, but also how I would theorize my work moving forward. In some anthropological work, particularly that where researchers are not racially or ethnically tied to the communities where they are working, grief serves as a wake-up call, a deepening of understanding of some aspect of the cultural context in which the work is taking place. Renato Rosaldo, for example, gives a detailed account of his wife's unexpected death during their fieldwork in the Philippines. It was this death that unlocked something for Rosaldo—a deeper understanding of how the community where he worked understood and experienced grief, validating the community's experiences.[12]

As a Black person in the United States, I often feel I am perpetually grieving, as the carceral state continues to demonstrate the extent to which Black lives are not valued. In the context of research, particularly in food studies where Black lives, Black communities, are central in conversations about food access and inequalities, grief as an experience and a methodological tool asked me to lean into the vulnerabilities that Faye Harrison argues are central to decolonizing anthropology.[13] In my experience, it was emotional and physical, but it was also intellectual in the sense that the grief was not separate from the joys and traumas of writing or conceiving an intellectual project. At the very least, grief challenged the age-old notion of "objectivity." At its most transformative, it radically changed how I saw, heard, and experienced the communities where I worked.

As interest in the political and economic aspects of food access increases, ethnographers potentially have much to contribute. My work is based on the assumption that anthropological practice should engage real-world problems, with the hopes of adding nuanced perspectives that will eventually lead to solutions. Setha Low defines "engaged anthropology" as "those activities that grow out of a commitment to the informants and communities with whom anthropologists work and a values-based stance that anthropological research respect the dignity and rights of all people and have a beneficent effect on the promotion of social justice."[14] What Low describes here is a form of anthropology that is separate from "regular" anthropology. But those following in the Black feminist anthropological tradition claim being engaged anthropologists as central to our understanding of the potential of the discipline. It is not separate or optional.

Food studies trained me to see connections between food access and neighborhoods, people and products. Black feminist theory, praxis, and living constantly teach me to see myself in the work, to experience my and others' wholeness, and to resist "objectivity" narratives in which grief has no place. In other words, it is when we bring our whole selves, with all the emotional and physical experiences that our fields may not have prepared us for, that we do the messy, hard work of getting free.

Caylon's life tottered at the intersections of food justice, economic justice, and racial justice as a formerly incarcerated Black man who was trying to reform his life but found himself challenged at multiple levels, sometimes unable to meet the needs of his family. He didn't simply talk about food justice; he lived it. He fed the homeless. He worked gardens. He advocated for more resources in neighborhoods like his. Yet, that work, that redemption, was not enough. As I (and others) consider research in food studies, we must also consider how food intersects with forms of oppression that influence or shape people's real lives. His work could not be extracted from his everyday lived experience. Neither could his death.

But we must also consider how these forms of oppression attempt to constrain us as researchers, how in some fields, like food studies, the very notion that the unexpected death of a research participant/friend/comrade is not considered—at least not methodologically or theoretically. It is a personal matter and not a public, professional one. But as is the case with many things, Black feminist theory and praxis shed a light on how to move forward. For me, that is to say: Black feminist theory and praxis give me tools, language, and permission to experience vulnerability as part of the work, not separate from it.

Black Food Futures

Much as Mr. Johnson and others shaped the direction of the fieldwork conducted for this book, Caylon's death, alongside the murders of Black women and men that gained national attention, deeply influenced how I think about the question, So what *are* the solutions? Residents in this study met their daily needs however they could, and their food geographies reveal the extent to which inequalities shape their lives. They did what the majority of us do: whatever it takes to meet their needs while making meaning of the conditions around them. Yet, as Caylon and others taught me, food was just one of the concerns that shaped their lives. These concerns varied—unequal food access, unstable housing, impending gentrification, crime, and economic precarity—but also stemmed from the same roots: racism. Where do we go when we put food in the context of Black liberation?

I do not pretend to know the answers to this question. What is clear, however, is that the global food regime, one in which components of our food system are in the hands of a few corporations, is not healthy for any of us. Within food, within the places where we purchase it, and within our consumption, we reproduce power structures that undergird the food inequalities highlighted in this book. We, too, have the potential to resist those power structures. Black people across space and time have tried to manage and combat the amount of harm those structures have done. Some marginal success is seen through Mr. Parker's store, the garden, and the ability to meet their food needs. That is what this book offers: a glimpse into what this self-reliance meant to residents; and perhaps it opens doors for thinking about self-reliance as a strategy for coalition and institution building.

Though this book is not about institutions or organizations, I come back to them as a necessary strategy moving forward, because food is never just about food. Neither is it solely about individual consumption. Perhaps best exhibited by the gardeners in chapter 5, self-reliance as a strategy is best realized through concerted, collective action that addresses multiple needs. On a small scale, this particular blueprint provides a way forward.

There are other examples. After eighteen years of having no grocery store, primarily Black residents in northeast Greensboro, North Carolina, pooled their resources and talents to open Renaissance Community Co-Op in 2016. With financial backing from diverse funders, Renaissance reflects what a belief in self-reliance can look like when residents collectively decide to reimagine their food environment. They did not wait for others to bring good food. They brought it themselves. By the time I was writing this book, residents of Ward 7 in D.C. were trying to organize a food co-op rather than waiting for a chain supermarket. For now, it is not clear how successful this will be, but it demonstrates residents' acknowledgment that the food inequities they navigate aren't individual problems and that collective action matters. For the National Black Food and Justice Alliance, a coalition of Black-led organizations, food sovereignty is integral to building Black futures and working toward liberation. Collectively, they imagine ways to grow food infrastructures to feed and sustain communities much like Deanwood. Their four-fold strategy—organizing people in Black communities, building visibility, directing action, and creating space for emerging collective wisdoms—is built on the assumption that anti-Blackness is killing us; and to survive, relationships to food, land, and each other must be healed.[15] Lastly, I'll highlight the Movement for Black Lives platform. Largely seen as a racial justice movement addressing police brutality, the platform, published online in 2016, indicates that the organizations that contributed to its development understand that racism and white supremacy are not limited to policing. The six-point platform addresses everything from an unjust judicial system to access to and control over land and food sources. All of these examples are blueprints for living and creating "in the wake." Christina Sharpe writes: "Living as I have argued we do in the wake of slavery, in spaces where we were never meant to survive, or have been punished for surviving and daring to claim or make spaces of something like freedom, we yet reimagine and transform spaces for and practices of an ethics of care (as in repair, maintenance, attention), an ethics of seeing, and of being in the wake as consciousness; as a way of remembering and observance that started with the door of no return, continued in the hold of the ship and on the shore."[16]

What does or would it mean for Ms. Johnson to flourish in the ways that she imagines for herself and community? More specifically, what does it mean to flourish in the context of anti-Blackness, displacement, and the constant reminders that for the maintenance of the state as it is currently articulated, Black lives have to *not* matter? What does it mean to rectify un/mattering through food, memory, nostalgia, and visions for self-reliance? Kim Q. Hall argues that "Good food . . . not only sustains life, it enables flourishing." Citing Chris Cuomo she further argues that flourishing is not about the self-reliant individual but only possible within community.[17] What is evident in the residents of Deanwood (and perhaps history and my own lived experience in a rural-born Black woman's body) is the "self" in self-reliant—when used by Black people—is hardly the individualist perspective imagined by enlightenment thinkers and beyond. Instead, "self" is already articulated as being enmeshed in community and perhaps this is where the possibilities lie. As we re/imagine our foodscapes near and far, one thing is clear: seeds of the food futures that are equitable and sustainable are in the stories, in the hopes, and in the lives of Black residents and organizations that look beyond what they can see and believe in something better.

Notes

Introduction

1. Reynolds and Cohen, *Beyond the Kale*, 3; Bandele and Myers, "The Roots of Black Agrarianism."

2. Vargas, *Catching Hell in the City of Angels*; Lipsitz, *How Racism Takes Place*; Woods, *Development Drowned and Reborn*.

3. McKittrick, "On Plantations, Prisons, and a Black Sense of Place."

4. Sharpe, *In the Wake*.

5. Bledsoe and Wright, "The anti-Blackness of Global Capital."

6. On October 7, 2014, Tina Campt delivered "Black Feminist Futures and the Practice of Fugitivity" at Barnard College as the Helen Pond McIntyre '48 Lecture.

7. McGranahan, "Theorizing Refusal," 319.

8. McGranahan, 322-23.

9. McClintock, "From Industrial Garden to Food Desert."

10. Illinois Advisory Committee to the U.S. Commission on Civil Rights, "Food Deserts in Chicago," Report of the Illinois Advisory Committee to the United States Commission on Human Rights, Chicago, October 2011. Accessed July 2, 2018, https://www.usccr.gov/pubs/docs/IL-FoodDeserts-2011.pdf.

11. Reynolds, "Disparity despite Diversity"; Kwate, Yau, et al., "Inequality in Obesigenic Environments."

12. "Low-income" tracts are defined as those where at least 20 percent of the population has income at or below the federal poverty levels for family size, or where the median family income for the tract is at or below 80 percent of the surrounding area's median family income. Tracts qualify as "low access" if at least 500 residents or 33 percent of their population live more than a mile from a supermarket or a large grocery store (for rural census tracts, the distance is more than ten miles).

13. Short, Guthman, and Raskin, "Food Deserts, Oases, or Mirages?"

14. Hunter and Robinson, *Chocolate Cities*; Hunter and Robinson, "The Sociology of Urban Black America"; Cox, *Shapeshifters*.

15. Raja and Yadav, "Beyond Food Deserts."

16. Agyeman and McEntee, "Moving the Field of Food Justice Forward through the Lens of Urban Political Ecology"; Morales, "Growing Food and Justice"; Guthman, "Bringing Good Food to Others."

17. Kwate, Loh, and White, "Retail Redlining in New York City," 634.

18. Alkon and Mares, "Food Sovereignty in US Food Movements," 353.

19. The Movement for Black Lives six-point platform includes demands for reparations, including "reparations for the wealth extracted from our communities through environmental racism, slavery, food apartheid, housing discrimination and racialized

capitalism in the form of corporate and government reparations, focused on healing ongoing physical and mental trauma, and ensuring our access and control of food sources, housing and land." For more information on The Movement for Black Lives policy platform, see https://policy.m4bl.org/platform/.

20. Brones, "Karen Washington."

21. Sbicca, "Growing Food Justice by Planting an Anti-Oppression Foundation," 461.

22. Bradley and Galt, "Practicing Food Justice at Dig Deep Farms and Produce, East Bay Area, California," 173.

23. Alkon et al., "Foodways of the Urban Poor"; Miewald and McCann, "Foodscapes and the Geographies of Poverty."

24. Ramirez, "The Elusive Inclusive."

25. McKittrick, *Demonic Grounds*.

26. McKittrick, "On Plantations, Prisons, and a Black Sense of Place."

27. Miewald and McCann, "Foodscapes and the Geographies of Poverty."

28. DuBois, *The Philadelphia Negro*.

29. DuBois, *The Souls of Black Folk*.

30. White, "'A Pig and a Garden.'"

31. Mullins, "Marketing in a Multicultural Neighborhood," 89.

32. McKittrick and Woods, "'No One Knows the Mysteries at the Bottom of the Ocean,'" 6.

33. Guthman, "Bringing Good Food to Others."

34. Williams-Forson, *Building Houses out of Chicken Legs*.

35. Broad, *More than Just Food*.

36. McCutcheon, "Food, Faith, and the Everyday Struggle for Black Urban Community"; McCutcheon, "Community Food Security 'for Us, by Us': The Nation of Islam and the Pan African Orthodox Christian Church," in *Cultivating Food Justice: Race, Class, and Sustainability*, ed. Alison Hope Alkon and Julian Agyeman (Cambridge, MA: MIT Press, 2011).

37. White, "D-Town Farm"; Reynolds and Cohen, *Beyond the Kale*.

38. Campt, "Black Feminist Futures and the Practice of Fugitivity."

39. Sampson, "Neighborhood-Level Context and Health."

40. Some participants were interviewed on multiple occasions. This was both to follow up on some of the factual information shared in the interview and to continue conversations that may have been cut short.

Chapter One

1. Neighborhood boundaries determined by the census cannot confine affect, movement, or attachment. As this book is as much about Black placemaking as about boundaries, the "official" boundaries mark the neighborhood for the purpose of understanding where supermarkets are located. The felt and affective boundaries, though, are understood much differently by residents, and not all agreed on what should or shouldn't be included as part of the neighborhood. In addition, because of migration patterns and connections across time and space, Marcus Hunter and Zandria Robinson argue that Black placemaking is always occurring in ways that

do not subscribe to traditional maps. See their 2018 book *Chocolate Cities* for a fuller discussion.

2. Overbeck and Chatmon, "Deanwood," 262.

3. Overbeck and Chatmon, 262.

4. Overbeck and Chatmon, 262.

5. Overbeck and Chatmon.

6. Crew, "Melding the Old and the New," 208.

7. Crew, 209.

8. Parks, "The Development of a Stable Black Community."

9. Gaines, *Uplifting the Race*, 1-2.

10. Prince, *African Americans and Gentrification in Washington, DC*; Crew, "Melding the Old and the New."

11. Crew, "Melding the Old and the New."

12. Parks, "The Development of a Stable Black Community," 10.

13. This map is from the John P. Wymer photograph collection housed at the Historical Society of Washington, D.C.'s Kiplinger Research Library (call number WY 0397M.08). The collection includes about 4,000 images of Washington, D.C., that were taken between 1948 and 1952. In addition to the description included on the map, Wymer includes this additional description of the land east of the Anacostia River: "About 30 percent of the land area of Washington lies east of the Anacostia River. Rather sketchily settled before World War II, it was[,] in 1948-50, the most rapidly growing section of the city. During the war and immediate postwar years, thousands of apartments and single family dwellings were built there. Nevertheless, even in 1950, there was still much vacant land left . . . Topographically, the area is one of the more attractive in the city. It is a region of gently rolling hills and valleys, with the many unexpected vistas of central Washington, and in the southern part, of Alexandria and the Potomac below Washington. The northern part of the area, depicted in this book[,] is inhabited almost exclusively by Negroes. South of this area, whites predominate, although there are several large sections dominated by Negroes."

14. Vincent Bunch interview, April 11, 1987, Series 6, box 19A, folder 7, MS2032, Ruth Ann Overbeck Papers & Washington Perspectives, Inc., Records, Special Collections Research Center, George Washington University, Washington, DC (hereafter cited as Ruth Ann Overbeck Papers).

15. Vincent Bunch interview.

16. Vincent Bunch interview.

17. Westmacott, *African-American Gardens*.

18. Parks, "The Development of a Stable Black Community," 7.

19. Westmacott, *African-American Gardens*, 192.

20. Deanwood History Committee, *Washington, DC's Deanwood*, 23.

21. Chin, *Purchasing Power*; Gregory, *Black Corona*.

22. Prince, *African Americans and Gentrification in Washington, D.C.*

23. Overbeck et al., "Final Report of Historical and Building Investigation of the Northeast Washington, D.C. Community of Deanwood, Phase I," 16.

24. Gregory, *Black Corona*, 54.

25. Parks, "The Development of a Stable Black Community," 6.

26. Parks, 7.

27. Community Market—the only Black-owned food store still located in Deanwood at the time of my fieldwork—was not mentioned at all in Overbeck's interviews, even though it opened in 1944, which was included in the time frame covered by the interviews. This was not because the first-generation owner was unknown in the community. On the contrary, respondents mentioned his other business—a carryout restaurant located on one of the main streets. The omission of Community Market suggests that it did not factor into residents' food procurement strategies.

28. Diner and Diner, "Washington's Jewish Community," 138.

29. Diner and Diner.

30. Jewish Historical Society of Greater Washington, "Half a Day on Sunday."

31. Brodkin, "How Did Jews Become White Folks?"

32. Kelly, "At Peak, District Grocery Stores Collective Comprised 300 Mom-and-Pop Shops."

33. Raspberry, "Small Stores Thrive through Cooperation."

34. Minnie Shumate Woodson—John Woodson Jr. interview, May 5, 1987, Series 6, box 19B, folder 4, MS2032, Ruth Ann Overbeck Papers.

35. Gottlieb and Joshi, *Food Justice*, 43; Certeau, Giard, and Mayol, *The Practice of Everyday Life*, vol. 2.

36. Dorothy M. Roberts interview, April 13, 1987, box 19A, folder 16, MS2032, Ruth Ann Overbeck Papers.

37. Dorothy Slaughter Dixon interview, April 16, 1987, Series 6, box 19A, folder 9, MS2032, Ruth Ann Overbeck Papers.

38. Emily Marin, taped interview, April 28, 1987, Series 6, box 19A, folder 15, MS2032, Ruth Ann Overbeck Papers.

39. Gottlieb and Joshi, *Food Justice*, 43.

40. Jones, "Supermarket Era Closes Cooperative."

41. Vargas, *Catching Hell in the City of Angels*, 35.

42. Whitehead, "The Formation of the U.S. Racialized Urban Ghetto," 5.

43. Prince, *African Americans and Gentrification in Washington, DC*.

44. Gregg, "The Grocery Stores' Flight to the Suburbs."

45. Gregg.

46. Jones, "Food Chains Reduce Operations in D.C."

47. Russell, "Black-Owned Grocery Chain Brings Service Back to NE Neighborhood."

48. Henderson and Hamilton, "Declining Population Saps D.C."

49. This data was assembled by a collective of researchers for NeighborhoodInfo DC, a project sponsored by the Urban Institute. Through a public website, NeighborhoodInfo DC seeks to "build the capacity of residents, community organizations, foundations, and local government to use data for decision making, program planning, and advocacy to improve the quality of life for low-income neighborhoods and residents in the District of Columbia and the Washington region." More information about the project, as well as D.C.-specific data (including data on individual wards), can be found at https://www.neighborhoodinfodc.org/index.html. Data from this source is cited as NeighborhoodInfo DC in subsequent notes.

50. NeighborhoodInfo DC.

51. NeighborhoodInfo DC.
52. NeighborhoodInfo DC.
53. Henderson and Hamilton, "Declining Population Saps D.C."
54. Gottlieb and Joshi, *Food Justice*.
55. "Are Minorities Neglected? Riots Put New Slant on Old Question," *Chain Store Age Executive*, July 1992; "Elderly and Poor Are Victims of Flight of the Supermarkets," *Washington Times*, November 16, 1992; Alix M. Freedman, "Poor Selection: An Inner-City Shopper Seeking Healthy Food Finds Offerings Scant," *Wall Street Journal*, December 20, 1990.
56. Russell, "Black-Owned Grocery Chain Brings Service Back to NE Neighborhood."
57. Millov, "Hill Grocer Succeeds Where Big Chains Fail."
58. Alix M. Dimock, "Inner-City Store Succeeds through Novel Ad Push," January 1982. I found a copy of this newspaper article, dated January 1982, in the archives at the Food Marketing Institute (in the box labeled "Store Location—Inner City), but the original source was not included. I was unable to find what newspaper it was originally published in. Searches in the local newspapers in Buffalo, New York, did not yield an answer.
59. Smith, "Hopes Outweigh Reality in PlazaMart Proposal."
60. Stoughton, "Grocery Chain Takes Pride in Selling to the Inner City."
61. Quoted in R. Sharpe, "Urban League Stresses Self-Reliance as Well as Jobs for Minorities in Report."
62. Mirabella, "Super Pride to Close All Stores."
63. Reed, "Super Pride Closing 3 Stores."
64. Reed.
65. Washington Post Staff Writer, "A Party with a Purpose."
66. NeighborhoodInfo DC.
67. Gregory, *Black Corona*, 55.

Chapter Two

1. Turshen, *Feed the Resistance*; Holt-Giménez and Harper, "Food-Systems-Racism"; McClintock, "From Industrial Garden to Food Desert."
2. Odoms-Young, Zenk, and Mason, "Measuring Food Availability and Access in African-American Communities"; Morland and Filomena, "Disparities in the Availability of Fruits and Vegetables between Racially Segregated Urban Neighbourhoods"; Zenk, "Neighborhood Racial Composition, Neighborhood Poverty, and the Spatial Accessibility of Supermarkets in Metropolitan Detroit."
3. Chung and Myers, "Do the Poor Pay More for Food?"
4. Williams and Collins, "Racial Residential Segregation"; Eisenhauer, "In Poor Health."
5. Hunter and Robinson, *Chocolate Cities*; Hunter and Robinson, "The Sociology of Urban Black America"; Taylor, *From #BlackLivesMatter to Black Liberation*; Cox, *Shapeshifters*.
6. Guthman, "Doing Justice to Bodies?"; Guthman, "Bringing Good Food to Others"; Kwate, "Fried Chicken and Fresh Apples."

7. Alkon et al., "Foodways of the Urban Poor"; Guthman, *Weighing In*.

8. FMI has various definitions for different stores. This number included only stores with $2 million or more in annual sales.

9. Asch and Musgrove, *Chocolate City*; Robinson, *This Ain't Chicago*; Kwate, "Fried Chicken and Fresh Apples"; Williams and Collins, "Racial Residential Segregation"; Low, "The Edge and the Center"; Prince, *African Americans and Gentrification in Washington, DC*.

10. Jaffe and Sherwood, *Dream City*, 21.

11. D.C. Hunger Solutions, "Closing the Grocery Store Gap in the Nation's Capital."

12. Massey and Denton, *American Apartheid*; Williams and Collins, "Racial Residential Segregation."

13. The Department of the Treasury's New Markets Tax Credit Program defines low-income neighborhoods as (a) census tracts with a poverty rate of 20 percent or greater; (b) census tracts with a median family income less than or equal to 80 percent of the statewide median family income; or (c) tracts in a metropolitan area that has a family median income less than or equal to 80 percent of the metro area's median family income.

14. Taylor, *From #BlackLivesMatter to Black Liberation*, 29.

15. Taylor, 29.

16. Cattell, "Poor People, Poor Places, and Poor Health," 1512.

17. Alkon et al., "Foodways of the Urban Poor."

18. Kwate, "The Race against Time."

19. Mohatt et al., "Historical Trauma as Public Narrative."

20. Charron-Chénier, "Race and Consumption," 16.

Chapter Three

1. Lipsitz, *How Racism Takes Place*, 52.

2. McKittrick, *Demonic Grounds*, 1-2.

3. Munoz, "Selling Nostalgia."

4. Munoz, 289.

5. Bailly, "Spatial Imaginary and Geography"; Watkins, "Spatial Imaginaries Research in Geography."

6. Lipsitz, *How Racism Takes Place*, 52.

7. Shircliffe, "'We Got the Best of That World,'" 62.

8. Mullins, "Marketing in a Multicultural Neighborhood," 88.

9. Wilson, "Capital's Need to Sell and Black Economic Development," 966.

10. Lacy, *Blue-Chip Black*; Pattillo, *Black on the Block*.

11. Boyd, *Jim Crow Nostalgia*.

12. On October 16, 1967, Federal Trade Commissioner Mary Gardiner Jones delivered a speech at the 34th Annual Meeting of the National Association of Food Chains entitled "The Revolution of Rising Expectations: The Ghetto's Challenge to American Business." The text of this speech was found in the archives at the Food Marketing Institute in Arlington, Virginia.

13. Coontz, *The Way We Never Were*, 85.

14. Though Cliff reported that his mother was a stay-at-home mother and wife, the reality was that for many Black families, even middle-class families, mothers worked outside the home to sustain the household. For more in-depth exploration of Black women's labor and work, see Tera Hunter's *To 'Joy My Freedom: Southern Black Women's Lives and Labor after the Civil War*, Stephanie Shaw's *What a Woman Ought to Be and to Do: Black Professional Women Workers during the Jim Crow Era*, and Riché Barnes's *Raising the Race: Black Career Women Redefine Marriage, Motherhood, and Community*.

15. Coontz, *The Way We Never Were*.

16. Hunter and Robinson, *Chocolate Cities*, 3.

17. Taylor, *From #BlackLivesMatter to Black Liberation*.

18. Shircliffe, "'We Got the Best of That World.'"

19. Quoted in Shircliffe, 62.

Chapter Four

1. Mullins, "Marketing in a Multicultural Neighborhood."

2. Gillette, *Between Justice and Beauty*.

3. Deanwood History Committee, *Washington, DC's Deanwood*, 56-57.

4. Gittelsohn et al., "B'More Healthy Communities for Kids"; Borradaile, Sherman, and Vander Veur, "Snacking in Children."

5. Chin, *Purchasing Power*.

6. Certeau, Giard, and Mayol, *The Practice of Everyday Life*, 2:81.

7. Vaught, "Cornering the Black Market," 3.

8. DeBonis, "Update: Marion Barry Apologizes for Anti-Asian Remarks."

9. DeBonis.

10. DeBonis.

11. Goldman, "Young to Quit Wal-Mart Group after Racial Remarks."

12. C. Lee, "Conflicts, Riots, and Korean Americans in Los Angeles, 1965-1992"; Wang, "Industrial Concentration of Ethnic Minority- and Women-Owned Businesses"; Min, "Changes in Korean Immigrants' Business Patterns"; J. Lee, "The Salience of Race in Everyday Life"; Youn, *Learning to Live and Work Together*.

13. C. Lee, "Conflicts, Riots, and Korean Americans in Los Angeles, 1965-1992."

14. Thompson, "The Moral Economy of the English Crowd in the Eighteenth Century," 78-79.

15. Palomera and Vetta, "Moral Economy: Rethinking a Radical Concept," 414.

16. Palomera and Vetta.

17. Wilson, "Capital's Need to Sell and Black Economic Development," 966.

18. Wilson.

19. Schwartzman, "Whose H Street Is It, Anyway?"

Chapter Five

1. Green Space is a pseudonym.

2. At the time I researched and wrote this book, many of the residents had moved from the housing projects, but others remained, and no construction was under way.

Other parts of the plan were visible in the neighborhood, though. For example, a new mixed-income apartment unit was near completion at the time of writing. In fact, that apartment building was being constructed in the once bare field across from Anne's house. The complete plan can be viewed at https://planning.dc.gov/publication /deanwood-strategic-development-plan-main-page.

3. McCormick, Joseph, and Chaskin, "The New Stigma of Relocated Public Housing Residents"; Darcy, "De-concentration of Disadvantage and Mixed Income Housing."

4. Poulsen, Hulland, and Gulas, "Growing an Urban Oasis."

5. Gregory, *Black Corona*; Prince, *African Americans and Gentrification in Washington, DC*.

6. Hunter and Robinson, *Chocolate Cities*.

Conclusion

1. Trauger, *We Want Land to Live*.

2. Guthman, *Weighing In*, 68.

3. Logan and Molotch, *Urban Fortunes*.

4. Sampson, "Neighborhood-Level Context and Health."

5. Trauger, *We Want Land to Live*.

6. Mintz, *Tasting Food, Tasting Freedom*.

7. Guthman, "Bringing Good Food to Others."

8. Bourdieu, *Distinction*.

9. Munoz, "Selling Nostalgia."

10. Vargas, *Never Meant to Survive*.

11. McClaurin, "Theorizing a Black Feminist Self in Anthropology."

12. Rosaldo, "Grief and a Headhunter's Rage."

13. On March 3, 2016, Faye Harrison sat down with Bianca Williams, Kaifa Roland, and Carole McGranahan for a conversation about decolonizing anthropology, during which she said that one thing that distinguishes anthropology from sociology, cultural geography, and other disciplines is a "participatory ethic." This requires us to be humble, vulnerable, and willing to reorient ourselves toward things we once thought we knew. A transcript of that conversation is available at https://savageminds.org/2016 /05/02/decolonizing-anthropology-a-conversation-with-faye-v-harrison-part-i/.

14. Low, "Claiming Space for an Engaged Anthropology," 390.

15. To read more about the National Black Food and Justice Alliance's theory, strategy, and platform visit their website: http://www.blackfoodjustice.org/rationale -strategy.

16. C. Sharpe, *In the Wake*, 130-31.

17. Hall, "Towards a Queer Crip Feminist Politics of Food," 178.

Bibliography

Agyeman, J., and J. McEntee. "Moving the Field of Food Justice Forward through the Lens of Urban Political Ecology." *Geography Compass* 8, no. 3 (2014): 211-20.

Alkon, Alison Hope, Daniel Block, Kelly Moore, Catherine Gillis, Nicole DiNuccio, and Noel Chavez. "Foodways of the Urban Poor." *Geoforum* 48 (2013): 126-35.

Alkon, Alison Hope, and Teresa Marie Mares. "Food Sovereignty in US Food Movements: Radical Visions and Neoliberal Constraints." *Agriculture and Human Values* 29, no. 3 (November 16, 2012): 347-59.

Asch, Chris Myers, and George Derek Musgrove. *Chocolate City: A History of Race and Democracy in the Nation's Capital*. Chapel Hill: University of North Carolina Press, 2017.

Bailly, Antoine Sylvain. "Spatial Imaginary and Geography: A Plea for the Geography of Representations." *GeoJournal* 31, no. 3 (1993): 247-50.

Bandele, Owusu, and Gail Myers. "The Roots of Black Agrarianism." Food First, 2012. https://foodfirst.org/wp-content/uploads/2016/08/DR4_final.pdf.

Barnes, Riché J. Daniel. *Raising the Race: Black Career Women Redefine Marriage, Motherhood, and Community*. New Brunswick, NJ: Rutgers University Press, 2015.

Bledsoe, Adam, and Willie Jamaal Wright. "The anti-Blackness of Global Capital." Environment and Planning D: Society and Space (2018): 1-19.

Borradaile, K. E., S. Sherman, and S. S. Vander Veur. "Snacking in Children: The Role of Urban Corner Stores." *Pediatrics* 124, no. 5 (2009): 1292-97.

Bourdieu, Pierre. *Distinction: A Social Critique of the Judgement of Taste*. Cambridge, MA: Harvard University Press, 1984.

Boyd, Michelle. *Jim Crow Nostalgia: Reconstructing Race in Bronzeville*. Minneapolis: University of Minnesota Press, 2008.

Bradley, Katharine, and Ryan E. Galt. "Practicing Food Justice at Dig Deep Farms & Produce, East Bay Area, California: Self-Determination as a Guiding Value and Intersections with Foodie Logics." *Local Environment* 19, no. 2 (2014): 172-86.

Broad, Garrett. *More Than Just Food: Food Justice and Community Change*. Berkeley: University of California Press, 2016.

Brodkin, Karen. "How Did Jews Become White Folks?" In *How Jews Became White Folks and What That Says about Race in America*, 25-52. New Brunswick, NJ: Rutgers University Press, 1998.

Brones, Anna. "Karen Washington: It's Not a Food Desert, It's Food Apartheid." *Guernica Magazine*, 2018. https://www.guernicamag.com/karen-washington-its-not-a-food-desert-its-food-apartheid/.

Campt, Tina. "Black Feminist Futures and the Practice of Fugitivity." Helen Pond McIntyre '48 Lecture, Barnard College, October 7, 2014. http://bcrw.barnard.edu/blog/black-feminist-futures-and-the-practice-of-fugitivity.

Cattell, Vicky. "Poor People, Poor Places, and Poor Health: The Mediating Role of Social Networks and Social Capital." *Social Science and Medicine* 52, no. 10 (May 2001): 1501-16.

Certeau, Michel de, Luce Giard, and Pierre Mayol. *The Practice of Everyday Life*. Vol. 2. Berkeley: University of California Press, 1998.

Charron-Chénier, Raphaël. "Race and Consumption: Consumer Markets and the Production of Racial Inequality." PhD diss., Duke University, 2017.

Chin, Elizabeth. *Purchasing Power: Black Kids and Consumer Culture*. Minneapolis: University of Minnesota Press, 2001.

Chung, Chanjin, and Samuel L. Myers. "Do the Poor Pay More for Food? An Analysis of Grocery Store Availability and Food Price Disparities." *Journal of Consumer Affairs* 33, no. 2 (December 3, 1999): 276-96.

Coontz, Stephanie. *The Way We Never Were: American Families and the Nostalgia Trap*. New York: Basic Books, 1993.

Cox, Aimee Meredith. *Shapeshifters: Black Girls and the Choreography of Citizenship*. Durham, NC: Duke University Press, 2015.

Crew, Spencer R. "Melding the Old and the New: The Modern African American Community, 1930-1960." In *Washington Odyssey: A Multicultural History of the Nation's Capital*, edited by Francine Cary, 208-27. Washington, DC: Smithsonian Books, 2003.

Darcy, Michael. "De-concentration of Disadvantage and Mixed Income Housing: A Critical Discourse Approach." *Housing, Theory and Society* 27, no. 1 (2010): 1-22.

D.C. Hunger Solutions. "Closing the Grocery Store Gap in the Nation's Capital." Washington, DC, 2016. Accessed July 2, 2018. http://www.dchunger.org/pdf/dchs-closing-grocery-store-gap-report.pdf.

Deanwood History Committee. *Washington, DC's Deanwood*. Charleston, SC: Arcadia Publishing, 2008.

DeBonis, Mike. "UPDATE: Marion Barry Apologizes for Anti-Asian Remarks." *Washington Post*, April 5, 2012.

Diner, Hasia R., and Steven J. Diner. "Washington's Jewish Community: Separate but Not Apart." In *Washington Odyssey: A Multicultural History of the Nation's Capital*. Washington, DC: Smithsonian Books, 1996.

DuBois, W. E. B. *The Philadelphia Negro: A Social Study*. Philadelphia: University of Pennsylvania Press, 1899.

——. *The Souls of Black Folk*. Tampa, FL: Millennium Publications, 2014.

Eisenhauer, Elizabeth. "In Poor Health: Supermarket Redlining and Urban Nutrition." *GeoJournal* 53, no. 2 (2001): 125-33.

Gaines, Kevin K. *Uplifting the Race: Black Leadership, Politics, and Culture in the Twentieth Century*. Chapel Hill: University of North Carolina Press, 1996.

Gillette, Howard. *Between Justice and Beauty: Race, Planning, and the Failure of Urban Policy in Washington, D.C.* Philadelphia: University of Pennsylvania Press, 1995.

Gittelsohn, Joel, Elizabeth Anderson Steeves, Yeeli Mui, Anna Y. Kharmats, Laura C. Hopkins, and Donna Dennis. "B'More Healthy Communities for Kids: Design of a Multi-level Intervention for Obesity Prevention for Low-Income African American Children." *BMC Public Health* 14 (2014): 942.

Goldman, Abigail. "Young to Quit Wal-Mart Group After Racial Remarks." *L.A. Times*, August 8, 2016.

Gottlieb, Robert, and Anupama Joshi. *Food Justice*. Cambridge, MA: MIT Press, 2010.

Gregg, Sandra R. "The Grocery Stores' Flight to the Suburbs." *Washington Post*, February 25, 1982.

Gregory, Steven. *Black Corona: Race and the Politics of Place in an Urban Community*. Princeton, NJ: Princeton University Press, 1999.

Guthman, Julie. "Bringing Good Food to Others: Investigating the Subjects of Alternative Food Practice." *Cultural Geographies* 15, no. 4 (October 1, 2008): 431–47.

———. "Doing Justice to Bodies? Reflections on Food Justice, Race, and Biology." *Antipode* 46, no. 5 (October 19, 2014): 1153–71.

———. *Weighing In: Obesity, Food Justice, and the Limits of Capitalism*. Berkeley: University of California Press, 2011.

Hall, Kim Q. "Toward a Queer Crip Feminist Politics of Food." *philoSOPHIA* 4, no. 2 (2014): 177–96.

Henderson, Nell, and Martha Hamilton. "Declining Population Saps D.C.: As Residents Leave, Age, City's Tax Base Withers." *Washington Post*, October 30, 1994.

Holt-Giménez, Eric, and Breeze Harper. "Food-Systems-Racism: From Mistreatment to Transformation." *Food First* 1, no. 1 (October 24, 2016): 1–7.

Hunter, Marcus Anthony, and Zandria F. Robinson. *Chocolate Cities: The Black Map of American Life*. Berkeley: University of California Press, 2018.

———. "The Sociology of Urban Black America." *Annual Review of Sociology* 42 (2016): 385–405.

Hunter, Tera W. *To 'Joy my Freedom: Southern Black Women's Lives and Labors after the Civil War*. Cambridge, MA: Harvard University Press, 1997.

Hurston, Zora Neale. *Dust Tracks on a Road*. New York: HarperPerennial, 1996.

Jaffe, Harry S., and Tom Sherwood. *Dream City: Race, Power, and the Decline of Washington, D.C.* New York: Simon and Schuster, 1994.

Jewish Historical Society of Greater Washington. "Half a Day on Sunday: Jewish-Owned 'Mom and Pop' Grocery Stores." 2007. https://www.jhsgw.org/exhibitions/online/momandpop/.

Jones, William H. "Food Chains Reduce Operations in D.C." *Washington Post*, April 1, 1971.

———. "Supermarket Era Closes Cooperative." *Washington Post*, November 13, 1972.

Kelly, John. "At Peak, District Grocery Stores Collective Comprised 300 Mom-and-Pop Shops." *Washington Post*, October 2, 2010.

Kwate, Naa Oyo A. "Fried Chicken and Fresh Apples: Racial Segregation as a Fundamental Cause of Fast Food Density in Black Neighborhoods." *Health and Place* 14, no. 1 (2008): 32–44.

———. "The Race Against Time: Lived Time, Time Loss, and Black Health Opportunity." *Du Bois Review: Social Science Research on Race* 14, no. 2 (2017): 497–514.

Kwate, Naa Oyo A., Ji Meng Loh, and Kellee White. "Retail Redlining in New York City: Racialized Access to Day-to-Day Retail Resources." *Journal of Urban Health* 90, no. 4 (2012): 632-53.

Kwate, Naa Oyo A., Chun Yip Yau, Ji Meng Loh, and Donya Williams. "Inequality in Obesigenic Environments: Fast Food Density in New York City." *Health and Place* 15, no. 1 (2009): 364-73.

Lacy, Karyn R. *Blue-Chip Black: Race, Class, and Status in the New Black Middle Class.* Berkeley: University of California Press, 2007.

Lee, Changaeng. "Conflicts, Riots, and Korean Americans in Los Angeles, 1965-1992." PhD Diss., Stony Brook University, 2012.

Lee, Jennifer. "The Salience of Race in Everyday Life: Black Customers' Shopping Experiences in Black and White Neighborhoods." *Work and Occupations* 27, no. 3 (2000): 353-76.

Lipsitz, George. *How Racism Takes Place.* Philadelphia: Temple University Press, 2011.

Logan, John R., and Harvey L. Molotch. *Urban Fortunes: The Political Economy of Place.* Berkeley: University of California Press, 1987.

Low, Setha M. "Claiming Space for an Engaged Anthropology: Spatial Inequality and Social Exclusion." *American Anthropologist* 113, no. 3 (2011): 389-407.

———. "The Edge and the Center: Gated Communities and the Discourse of Urban Fear." *American Anthropologist* 103, no. 1 (1998): 45-58.

Massey, Douglas S., and Nancy A. Denton. *American Apartheid: Segregation and the Making of the Underclass.* Cambridge, MA: Harvard University Press, 1993.

McClaurin, Irma. "Theorizing a Black Feminist Self in Anthropology: Toward an Autoethnographic Approach." In *Black Feminist Anthropology: Theory, Politics, Praxis, and Poetics*, edited by Irma McClaurin, 49-76. New Brunswick, NJ: Rutgers University Press, 2001.

McClintock, Nathan. "From Industrial Garden to Food Desert: Demarcated Devaluation in the Flatlands of Oakland, California." In *Cultivating Food Justice: Race, Class, and Sustainability*, edited by Alison Hope Alkon and Julian Agyeman, 89-120. Cambridge, MA: MIT Press, 2011.

McCormick, Naomi J., Mark L. Joseph, and Robert J. Chaskin. "The New Stigma of Relocated Public Housing Residents: Challenges to Social Identity in Mixed-income Developments." *City & Community* 11, no. 3 (2012): 285-308.

McCutcheon, Priscilla. "Community Food Security 'for Us, by Us': The Nation of Islam and the Pan African Orthodox Christian Church." In *Cultivating Food Justice: Race, Class, and Sustainability*, edited by Alison Hope Alkon and Julian Agyeman, 177-96. Cambridge, MA: MIT Press, 2011.

———. "Food, Faith, and the Everyday Struggle for Black Urban Community." *Social & Cultural Geography* 16, no. 4 (2015): 385-406.

McGranahan, Carole. "Theorizing Refusal: An Introduction." *Cultural Anthropology* 31, no. 3 (2016): 319-25.

McKittrick, Katherine. *Demonic Grounds: Black Women and the Cartographies of Struggle.* Minneapolis: University of Minnesota Press, 2006.

———. "On Plantations, Prisons, and a Black Sense of Place." *Social and Cultural Geography* 12, no. 8 (2011): 947-63.

McKittrick, Katherine, and Clyde Woods. "'No One Knows the Mysteries at the Bottom of the Ocean.'" In *Black Geographies and the Politics of Place*, edited by Katherine McKittrick and Clyde Woods, 1-13. Cambridge, MA: South End Press, 2007.

Miewald, Christiana, and Eugene McCann. "Foodscapes and the Geographies of Poverty: Sustenance, Strategy, and Politics in an Urban Neighborhood." *Antipode* 46, no. 2 (2014): 537-56.

Millov, Courtland. "Hill Grocer Succeeds Where Big Chains Fail." *Washington Post*, January 31, 1980.

Min, Pyon Gap. 2012. "Changes in Korean Immigrants' Business Patterns." In *Koreans in North America: Their Experiences in the Twenty-First Century*, edited by Pyong Gap Min. Lanham, MD: Lexington Books.

Mintz, Sidney. *Tasting Food, Tasting Freedom: Excursions into Eating, Power, and the Past*. Boston: Beacon Press, 1996.

Mirabella, Lorraine. "Super Pride to Close All Stores." *Baltimore Sun*, October 3, 2000.

Mohatt, Nathaniel Vincent, Azure B. Thompson, Nghi D. Thai, and Jacob Kraemer Tebes. "Historical Trauma as Public Narrative: A Conceptual Review of How History Impacts Present-Day Health." *Social Science and Medicine* 106 (2014): 128-36.

Morales, Alfonso. "Growing Food and Justice: Dismantling Racism through Sustainable Food Systems." In *Cultivating Food Justice: Race, Class, and Sustainability*, edited by Alison Hope Alkon and Julian Agyeman, 149-76. Cambridge, MA: MIT Press, 2011.

Morland, Kimberly, and Susan Filomena. "Disparities in the Availability of Fruits and Vegetables between Racially Segregated Urban Neighbourhoods." *Public Health Nutrition* 10, no. 12 (2007): 1481-89.

Mullins, Paul R. "Marketing in a Multicultural Neighborhood: An Archaeology of Corner Stores in the Urban Midwest." *Historical Archaeology* 42, no. 1 (2008): 88-96.

Munoz, Lorena. "Selling Nostalgia: The Emotional Labor of Immigrant Latina Food Vendors in Los Angeles." *Food and Foodways* 25, no. 4 (2017): 283-99.

Odoms-Young, Angela M., Shannon Zenk, and Maryann Mason. "Measuring Food Availability and Access in African-American Communities: Implications for Intervention and Policy." *American Journal of Preventive Medicine* 36, no. 4 (2009): S145-50.

Overbeck, Ruth Ann, and Kia Chatmon. "Deanwood: Self-Reliance at the Eastern Point." In *Washington at Home: An Illustrated History of Neighborhoods in the Nation's Capital*, 2nd ed., edited by Kathryn Schneider Smith, 257-72. Baltimore: Johns Hopkins University Press, 2010.

Overbeck, Ruth Ann, Laura Henley, J. V. Lee, Julia Parks, John Ross, and Robert Verrey. "Final Report of Historical and Building Investigation of the Northeast

Washington, D.C. Community of Deanwood, Phase I." Ruth Ann Overbeck's Papers. Washington, DC: George Washington University, 1987.

Palomera, Jaime, and Theodora Vetta. "Moral Economy: Rethinking a Radical Concept." *Anthropological Theory*, no. 4 (December 2016): 413-32.

Parks, Julia. "The Development of a Stable Black Community: Report on an Oral History of Deanwood." Ruth Ann Overbeck's Papers. Washington, DC: George Washington University, 1987.

Pattillo, Mary. *Black on the Block: The Politics of Race and Class in the City*. Chicago: University of Chicago Press, 2007.

Poulsen, Melissa N., Kristyna R. S. Hulland, Carolyn A. Gulas, Hieu Pham, Sarah L. Dalglish, Rebecca K. Wilkinson, and Peter J. Winch. "Growing an Urban Oasis: A Qualitative Study of the Perceived Benefits of Community Gardening in Baltimore, Maryland." *Culture, Agriculture, Food and Environment* 36, no. 2 (2014): 69-82.

Prince, Sabiyha. *African Americans and Gentrification in Washington, DC: Race, Class and Social Justice in the Nation's Capital*. Farnham, UK: Ashgate Publishing, 2014.

Raja, Samina, Changxing Ma, and Pavan Yadav. "Beyond Food Deserts: Measuring and Mapping Racial Disparities in Neighborhood Food Environments." *Journal of Planning Education and Research* 27, no. 4 (January 24, 2008): 469-82.

Ramirez, Margaret Marietta. "The Elusive Inclusive: Black Food Geographies and Racialized Food Spaces." *Antipode* 47, no. 3 (2015): 748-69.

Raspberry, William. "Small Stores Thrive through Cooperation." *Washington Post*, February 10, 1963.

Reed, Keith T. "Super Pride Closing 3 Stores." *Baltimore Business Journal*, June 26, 2000.

Reynolds, Kristin. "Disparity despite Diversity: Social Injustice in New York City's Urban Agriculture System." *Antipode* 47, no 1 (2015): 240-59.

Reynolds, Kristin, and Nevin Cohen. *Beyond the Kale: Urban Agriculture and Social Justice Activism in New York City*. Athens: University of Georgia Press, 2016.

Robinson, Zandria F. *This Ain't Chicago: Race, Class, and Regional Identity in the Post-Soul South*. Chapel Hill: University of North Carolina Press, 2014.

Rosaldo, Renato. "Grief and a Headhunter's Rage." *Death, Mourning, and Burial: A Cross-cultural Reader* (2004): 167-78.

Russell, Brenda A. "Black-Owned Grocery Chain Brings Service Back to NE Neighborhood." *Washington Post*, July 2, 1981.

Sampson, Robert J. "Neighborhood-Level Context and Health: Lessons from Sociology." In *Neighborhoods and Health*, edited by Ichiro Kawachi and Lisa F. Berkman, 132-46. Oxford: Oxford University Press, 2003.

Sbicca, Joshua. "Growing Food Justice by Planting an Anti-Oppression Foundation: Opportunities and Obstacles for a Budding Social Movement." *Agriculture and Human Values* 29, no. 4 (November 14, 2012): 455-66.

Schwartzman, Paul. "Whose H Street Is It, Anyway?" *Washington Post*, April 4, 2006.

Sharpe, Christina. *In the Wake: On Blackness and Being*. Durham, NC: Duke University Press, 2016.

Sharpe, Rochelle. "Urban League Stresses Self-Reliance as Well as Jobs for Minorities in Report." *Wall Street Journal*, January 21, 1994.

Shaw, Stephanie J. *What a Woman Ought to Be and to Do: Black Professional Women Workers During the Jim Crow Era*. University of Chicago Press, 2010.

Shircliffe, Barbara. "'We Got the Best of That World': A Case for the Study of Nostalgia in the Oral History of School Segregation." *The Oral History Review* 28, no. 2 (2001): 59-84.

Short, A., J. Guthman, and S. Raskin. "Food Deserts, Oases, or Mirages? Small Markets and Community Food Security in the San Francisco Bay Area." *Journal of Planning Education and Research* 26, no. 3 (March 1, 2007): 352-64.

Smith, Starita. "Hopes Outweigh Reality in PlazaMart Proposal." *Columbus Dispatch*, June 16, 1985.

Stoughton, Stephanie. "Grocery Chain Takes Pride in Selling to the Inner City." *Washington Times*, August 2, 1993.

Taylor, Keeanga-Yamahtta. *From #BlackLivesMatter to Black Liberation*. Chicago: Haymarket Books, 2016.

Thompson, E.P. "The Moral Economy of the English Crowd in the Eighteen Century." *Past & Present*, no. 50 (February 1971): 76-136.

Trauger, Amy. *We Want Land to Live: Making Political Space for Food Sovereignty*. University of Georgia Press, 2017.

Turshen, Julia. *Feed the Resistance: Recipes + Ideas for Getting Involved*. San Francisco: Chronicle Books, 2017.

Vargas, Joao H. Costa. *Catching Hell in the City of Angels: Life and Meanings of Blackness in South Central Los Angeles*. Minneapolis: University of Minnesota Press, 2006.

———. *Never Meant to Survive: Genocide and Utopias in Black Diaspora Communities*. New York: Rowman and Littlefield, 2008.

Vaught, Seneca. "Cornering the Black Market: A Role for the Corner Store in Community Development." Fourth World Conference on Remedies to Racial and Ethnic Economic Inequality, 2012.

Wang, Qingfang. "Industrial Concentration of Ethnic Minority- and Women-Owned Businesses: Evidence from the Survey of Business Owners in the United States." *Journal of Small Business and Entrepreneurship* 26, no. 3 (2013): 299-321.

Washington Post Staff Writer. "A Party with a Purpose: Antidrug Rally Set in Scarred NE Area." *Washington Post*, July 9, 1987.

Watkins, Josh. "Spatial Imaginaries Research in Geography: Synergies, Tensions, and New Directions." *Geography Compass* 9 (2015): 508-22.

Westmacott, Richard. *African-American Gardens: Yards in Rural South*. Knoxville: University of Tennessee Press, 1992.

White, Monica M. "D-town Farm: African American Resistance to Food Insecurity and the Transformation of Detroit." *Environmental Practice* 13, no. 4 (2011): 406-17.

———. "'A Pig and a Garden': Fannie Lou Hamer and the Freedom Farms Cooperative." *Food and Foodways* 25, no. 1 (2017): 20-39.

Whitehead, Tony L. "The Formation of the U.S. Racialized Urban Ghetto." 2015. http://www.culturalsystemsanalysisgroup.umd.edu/documents/WorkingPapers/RUGOne.pdf.

Williams, David R., and Chiquita Collins. "Racial Residential Segregation: A Fundamental Cause of Racial Disparities in Health." *Public Health Reports* 116 (2001): 404-16.

Williams-Forson, Psyche A. *Building Houses Out of Chicken Legs: Black Women, Food, and Power*. Chapel Hill: University of North Carolina Press, 2006.

Wilson, Bobby M. "Capital's Need to Sell and Black Economic Development." *Urban Geography* 33, no. 7 (2012): 961-78.

Woods, Clyde. *Development Drowned and Reborn: The Blues and Bourbon Restorations in Post-Katrina New Orleans*. Edited by Jordan T. Camp and Laura Pulido. Athens: University of Georgia Press, 2017.

Youn, ChangGook. *Learning to Live and Work Together: Coalition Building among Korean Merchants Groups, Community Residents, and Community Organizations*. PhD diss., Pennsylvania State University, 2007.

Zenk, Shannon N., Amy J. Schulz, Barbara A. Israel, Sherman A. James, Shuming Bao, and Mark L. Wilson. "Neighborhood Racial Composition, Neighborhood Poverty, and the Spatial Accessibility of Supermarkets in Metropolitan Detroit." *American Journal of Public Health* 95, no. 4 (2005): 660-67.

Index

Page numbers in italics refer to figures. Page numbers in italics, followed by "m," refer to maps. Page numbers in italics, followed by "t," refer to tables.

access to food: changes in, 42–43; "food desert" term and, 5–7; health and, 5, 58, 60–62, 64–66; nuances of, 131–33; overview of, 5; self-reliance and, 8–12, 42, 134; spatiality and, 5, 6, 8–9, 132; surveys and, 15

activism, food, 9–10, 11, 46

agency, Black: community garden and, 122, 129, 130; at neighborhood level, 42, 131, 132; self-reliance and, 8, 11

Alkon, Alison Hope, 7, 60

alternative food movements, 46, 66, 74, 132

Anacostia River, 47–48, 51

Anne (Deanwood resident), 27, 55, 58, 74–80, 88, 89–90

anthropologists, black women, 134–35

anthropology, 134–36, 148n13

anti-Blackness: as an analytic, 3–4; Deanwood and, 73; food system and, 5–7; migration and, 21–22, 45. *See also* racism

apartments, mixed-income, 115, 147n2

archival research, 14

Asian-owned businesses, 100–101, 103–4

Barry, Marion, 100–101

bartering and trading, 27–28

Beall, Ninian, 20

black economy, 73, 105

"Black Feminist Futures and the Practice of Fugitivity" (Campt), 4

Black feminist theory, 134, 136, 137

Black food geographies overview, 8, 11–12

"black ghettoes," 34–35

Black-owned businesses, 29, *30m*, 33, 103, 105–6, 108, 144n27. *See also* Community Market; Super Pride

Bledsoe, Adam, 4

boundaries, neighborhood, 19, 142–43n1

Bourdieu, Pierre, 133

Boyd, Michelle, 79

Bradley, Katharine, 7

bricks, dumped, *120*, 120–21

budgeting, 62–65

Bunch, Vincent, 24–26

Burley, John H. W., 20

Burns, Charles T., 38

Burroughs, Nannie Helen, 10, 21, 115, 129

Burrville School, 21

Butler, Octavia, 69–70

Campt, Tina, 141n6; "Black Feminist Futures and the Practice of Fugitivity" and, 4

capital, 105

capitalism, 105–6

Cattell, Vicky, 59

Caylon, 44–45, 61–62, 134, 135, 136–37

Certeau, Michel de, 97–98

change: in community, 42, 79, 80–83, 106–9; in food systems, 26–27, 33, 43, *50t*, 83; nostalgia and, 80–83; in populations, 37, 41

Charron-Chénier, Raphaël, 67–68

children: community garden and, 111, 126–28; Community Market and, 96–97, 98; food decisions and, 60–65; obesity and, 127

Chin, Elizabeth, 96
churches in Deanwood, 78
civil rights legislation, 81
Cliff (Deanwood community leader),
    71–74, 80–83, 103–4
Collins, Chiquita, 45
community center at Deanwood, 14,
    115. *See also* community garden at
    Deanwood
community cohesion: grocery stores
    and, 59, 98–99; nostalgia and, 70–71,
    72–73, 79, 84, 104; self-reliance and,
    28, 42; trading and bartering and,
    27–28
community garden at Deanwood, 14,
    124; Community Planting Day and,
    111–14; makeshift greenhouse and,
    114–18, *117*; needs addressed by,
    123–30; responsibility and, 119–23,
    120; start and purpose of, 118–19
Community Market: about, 91–97, *92*,
    104, 144n27; as an in-between space,
    101–2; change and transition and,
    99–100, 107, 108–9; community place
    of, 98–99, 102, 109–10; data collection
    and, 13–14; moral economy of, 104,
    106; racialization and, 105
Community Planting Day and Health
    Fair, 111–14, *112–13*
consumption, food, 67–68, 133
Coontz, Stephanie, 82, 85
Cooper, Anna Julia, 10
crack cocaine, 40–42
credit system, 31–33

Dametria (Deanwood resident), 56–57,
    62–64, 65, 86–88, 122–23, 125
Daron (Deanwood resident), 41–42,
    65–66, 69, 83, 85–89, 98–99, 103
data collection, 12–15
Deamber (community garden volunteer),
    126–27
Deanwood: about, 19, *23m*, 78, 143n13;
    as a community, 72–74; data collection
    and, 14–15; drugs and, 40–42;

economy of, 26, 27; grocery stores in,
    28–30, *30m. See also specific grocery
    stores*; history of, 20–24, 143n13;
    isolation of, 37; populations in,
    29–31, 41; self-reliance and, 22,
    84–86; transition of, 106
Deanwood Strategic Plan, 113–14,
    147–48n2
deaths, Black, 3–4
decision making, 59–60, 66, 67, 133
decolonizing anthropology, 136, 148n13
deindustrialization, 34
delis, 72, 106–7
desegregation, 79–80, 81, 83–84
Deshun, 126–27
DGS (District Grocery Store). *See*
    District Grocery Store (DGS)
disinvestment, 3, 19, 34, 113–14
distinction and food landscapes, 57–58
District Grocery Store (DGS), 31, 32, 34, 72
Dixon, Dorothy Slaughter, 32, 33
drugs, 40–42
DuBois, W. E. B., 9
Dust Tracks on the Road (Hurston), 2–3

Economic Research Service (ERS), 5–6
economy, black, 73, 105
Eisenhauer, Elizabeth, 6, 45
engaged anthropology, 136
entrepreneurship: black economy and,
    73, 105; community and, 93, 119,
    124–25; in Deanwood, 29–31; food
    stores and, 38–39, 42–43; as a
    strategy, 10, 28
ERS (Economic Research Service).
    See Economic Research Service (ERS)
ethnographic research at neighborhood
    level, 131–32

family units, 82
farming, 24, 25, 42, 46
feminist theory, Black, 134, 136, 137
FFC (Freedom Farm Cooperative).
    See Freedom Farm Cooperative (FFC)
fieldwork of author, 13, 16

flourishing as a metaphor, 122, 129, 139
FMI (Food Marketing Institute).
    See Food Marketing Institute (FMI)
Food Access Research Atlas, 5–6
food apartheid, 7, 141n19
food chains. *See* supermarkets
food co-ops, 138
food desert, term of, 5–7, 46, 67
food inequities: health and, 16, 45;
    spatiality and, 8, 11, 47–49, 48m, 49m,
    50t, 51, 133
food justice, 3–4, 11, 18, 46, 52, 138
Food Marketing Institute (FMI), 46,
    145n58, 146n8
food stores. *See* grocery stores, small;
    supermarkets
food studies, 2, 46, 132, 136–37
food systems: changes in, 26–27, 33, 43,
    50t, 83; race and, 3–4, 5–7, 45–46;
    systematic failures of, 51, 132
foodways, Black, 8–9, 11, 39, 66
Freedom Farm Cooperative (FFC), 10
future of Black food, 137–39

Gaines, Kevin, 22
Galt, Ryan, 7
gardening, 24–28, 74, 85, 134. *See also*
    community garden at Deanwood
gender roles, 82–83
general stores, 25, 99
gentrification, 52, 71, 80, 106, 108
geographies of self-reliance, term of, 8–9,
    11, 12
geography, 3, 60
Giant, 38, 40, 72
Giard, Luce, 97–98
global food regime, 137
Great Migration, 20, 21, 86
greenhouse, makeshift, 114–18, 117
Green Space, 111–13, 147n1
green tomatoes, 1
Gregg, Sandra R., 37
Gregory, Steven, 28, 130
grief, 134, 135–36
grocery stores, large. *See* supermarkets

grocery stores, small: Black-owned,
    38–40; in Deanwood, 28–33, 30m;
    racialization of, 99–104; as significant
    places, 97–98; sizes of, 34. *See also*
    Community Market
grocery walk protest, 52
Groceteria, 30m
growing food. *See* farming; gardening
Guthman, Julie, 131

Hall, Kim Q., 139
Hamer, Fannie Lou, 10
Harris, Mr. (community garden orga-
    nizer): community garden and, 99,
    111, 114–21, 124, 125, 127–28; grocery
    shopping and, 58–60; health and, 64–65
Harrison, Faye, 136, 148n13
Haynes, Cliff, 71–74, 80–83, 103–4
health: children's choices and, 96–97;
    community garden and, 119, 123, 129;
    Community Planting Day and Health
    Fair and, 111–13, 113; disparities in,
    45, 60; food access and, 5, 58, 60–62,
    64–66; food inequities and, 16, 45
High's, 77
Hinds, Aisha, 131
Historical Society of Washington, D. C.,
    14, 143n13
home ownership, 21–22, 24
housing projects of Deanwood, 86, 88,
    112, 115, 129, 147n2. *See also*
    community garden at Deanwood
hucksters, 26, 27
Hunter, Marcus, 85–86, 130, 142–43n1
Hurston, Zora Neale, 2–3

imaginaries, 70–71, 83, 86, 89–90, 94, 133
income, grocery store locations by,
    49m, 50t
individual responsibility, 56–57, 65, 107
industrialization, 42
inequities in food system. *See* food
    inequities
inspiration for this book, 15
integration, 79–80, 81, 83–84

interviews for this study, about, 12–13, 142n10
Irma (Deanwood resident), 52–53, 55
isolation of urban neighborhoods, 22, 34–35, 37, 47

Jaffe, Harry, 47, 51
Janice (Deanwood resident), 60–61, 84–85, 102, 110
Jewish immigrants, 29–31
Jewish-owned food stores, 29–33, 30m, 77
joblessness, 124
Johnson, Johnathan, 39
Johnson, Mr. (Deanwood resident), 1–2
Johnson, Ms. (president of the resident council): about, 113, 115; community and, 99; community garden and, 118–19, 121–22, 125, 127–28, 129
Jones, Mary Gardiner, 82, 146n12
Jones, Mr. (Community Market owner): about, 91–95, 98; change and, 106–10; community care of, 98–99; as a shopkeeper, 95–97
Joshua (head of agriculture in community garden), 113, 125–28

Kaba, Mariame, 131
Karen (Deanwood resident), 91
Kim (Deanwood resident), 57–58
Kindred (Butler), 69–70
Koti (Deanwood resident), 60–61, 84, 98, 99
Kwate, Naa Oyo, 6–7, 60

Lacy, Karyn, 76
landownership, 20, 25. *See also* home ownership
Lee, Chanhaeng, 104
Let's Move! campaign, 127
Lipsitz, George, 69, 70–71
Loh, Ji Meng, 6–7
Low, Setha, 136
low-income neighborhoods: defined, 52, 141n12, 146n13; food access and, 5–6, 131

Ma, Changxing, 6
macro-level processes, 45, 131, 132
Malcolm (community garden volunteer), 126–27
mapping tools, 5–6
maps: of Deanwood, 22–23, 23m, 30m, 143n13; of Washington D. C. area, 47–49, 48m, 49m
Mares, Teresa, 7
Marin, Emily, 32–33
Marvin Gaye Park, 41
Mayol, Pierre, 97–98
M4BL (Movement for Black Lives). *See* Movement for Black Lives (M4BL)
McClaurin, Irma, 134
McDonald's, 81, 103
McGranahan, Carole, 4
McKittrick, Katherine, 10–11, 69–70
memories, 69–70. *See also* nostalgia
methodology of this study, 12
migration, 20, 21, 34, 35, 37–38, 79, 86
Mintz, Sidney, 132
moral economies, 104–6
mother tongue, 118
Movement for Black Lives (M4BL), 7, 138, 141–42n19
Mullins, Paul, 10, 73, 93
Munoz, Lorena, 70, 133

National Black Food and Justice Alliance, 138
National Training School for Women and Girls, 10, 21
NeighborhoodInfo DC, 144n49
Newsweek, 6
Noon, Henry, 31, 34
Norton, Eleanor Holmes, 101
nostalgia: Anne and, 74, 75–80; Cliff Haynes and, 71–74, 80–83; overview of, 69–71, 89–90, 133; racialized responsibility and, 86–89; self-reliant community and, 84–86
nothingness, 9, 19, 44–47, 51, 57

Obama, Michelle, 122–23, 127
objectivity, 134, 136
Office of Planning, D. C., 113
oral histories, 90. *See also* oral history interviews of Ruth Ann Overbeck
oral history interviews of Ruth Ann Overbeck: about, 14–15, 21; small grocers and, 28, 29, *30m*, 31–35, 144n27
out-migration, 34, 35, 37–38, 79
Overbeck, Ruth Ann: about, 14, 21; oral history interviews of, 90. *See* oral history interviews of Ruth Ann Overbeck

Palomera, Jaime, 105
Parks, Julia, 26, 29
participant observations, 12, 13–14, 112
Pattillo, Mary, 76
personal responsibility, 56–57, 65, 107
place-making, 8, 10–11, 18, 142–43n1
populations: of Deanwood, 29, 31, 41; grocery store locations by, *48m*; of Washington, D. C., 21, 29, 37–38
Portellie, Alessandro, 90
Poulsen, Melissa N., 123
power structures, 137
precarity, 132–33, 134
Prince, Sabiyha, 35, 130
produce, selling from homes or carts, 26
"productive nostalgia," 70

quiet food refusals, 5
quiet photography, 4

race and food systems, 3–4, 5–7, 45–46
racialization: of food, 66; of grocery stores, 66, 99–104, 105; of responsibility, 86–89
"racialized urban ghettos," 34–37
racial uplift, 22
racism, 3–4, 7, 88, 90
Raja, Samina, 6

Ramirez, Margaret, 8
recreation center in Deanwood, 13, 16
redlining, supermarket, 6–7, 45–46
refusal, 4–5, 11, 12, 114, 133
relationships, community: black economy and, 105; grocers and, 27, 31–32, 74, 109–10; procuring food and, 59–60
Renaissance Community Co-op, 138
reparations, 141–42n19
respectability politics, 10, 22, 95
responsibility: communal, 94, 99, 109; community garden and, 123, 128, 129; individual, 56, 65, 97, 107–8; racialization of, 86–89
riots, 34, 104
Roberts, Dorothy M., 31–32
Robinson, Zandria, 85–86, 130, 142–43n1
Rosaldo, Renato, 135

Safeway: about, 13, 14, 19, 37, 38, 39, 48; Anne on, 76, 77; closings of, 37; in food access survey, 52–55, *54t*; quality and, 51–52
Sampson, Robert, 12
Sbicca, Joshua, 7
scholars, Black women, 134–35
scholarship on food access, 6–7, 9–10, 11, 45–46
segregation, residential, 9, 23, 45–47, 71, 73, 80, 81
self-reliance: community and, 26, 28, 56, 88, 109, 133; Community Market and, 94; Deanwood and, 22, 84–86; family unit and, 82; food access and, 8–9, 42, 134; food stores and, 39; gardening and, 25–26, 129–30; nostalgia and, 73, 74, 79, 80, 134; overview of, 8–12; as a strategy, 137–39; systematic failures and, 89. *See also* responsibility
Sharpe, Christina, 4, 138–39
Shaw, Washington D. C., 22
Sherwood, Tom, 47
Singletary Plaza Mart, 38

SNMA (Student National Medical Association). *See* Student National Medical Association (SNMA)

social networks, 58–59

socioeconomic status and food, 57–58, 68, 109

soul food, 40, 103

spatial imaginary, 70–71

spatiality: community garden and, 129; food access and, 5, 6, 8–9, 132; inequities and, 8, 11, 47–49, 48–49*m*, 50*t*, 51, 133; nostalgia and, 69–71, 74

Spic N Span, 77, 78

storytelling, Black, 2–3, 69

stressors, 58, 60

Student National Medical Association (SNMA), 111–12, *113*

studies on food consumption, 67–68

supermarkets: about, 33–34, 46, 132; capitalism and, 105–6; closings of, *35*, 36–37, 38–40; Community Foods, 28; Giant, 38, 40, 72; impact on community practices of, 27; locations of, 47–49, 48–49*m*; redlining of, 6–7, 45–46; Super Pride, 38, *39*, 39–40, 40, 55, 76, 78; Wegman's, 54, 55. *See also* Safeway

Super Pride, 38, *39*, 39–40, 40, 55, 76, 78

survey on food access, 15, 52–55, *53t*

systematic failures, 51, 88–89

Taylor, Keeanga-Yamahtta, 56–57, 89

"Theorizing a Black Feminist Self in Anthropology" (McClaurin), 134–35

Thompson, E. P., 104

time, 60

trading and bartering, 27–28

unequal spatial geography, 47–49, 48*m*, 49*m*, 50*t*, 51

United States Department of Agriculture (USDA), 5–6

uplift, community, 9–10, 22, 56

uprisings of 1968, 34

USDA (United States Department of Agriculture). *See* United States Department of Agriculture (USDA)

Vargas, Joao, 133

Vaught, Seneca, 100

Vetta, Theodora, 105

Walmart, 79–80

Washington, Booker T., 9

Washington, D. C.: as an unequal food landscape, 47–51; populations of, 21, 35, 37–38; wards of, *30m*, 37, 47

Washington, Karen, 7

Washington Post: on drugs, 41; on food stores, 31, 34, *35*, 37, 39–40; on Washington D.C., population, 37–38

Washington Post and Times-Herald, 35

Wegman's, 54, 55

Whitehead, Tony, 34–35

Williams, David, 45

Wilson, Bobby, 73, 105

work, shopping as, 58

Wright, Willie, 4

Wymer, John P., 23, 143n13

Yadav, Pavan, 6

Young, Andrew, 101

CPSIA information can be obtained
at www.ICGtesting.com
Printed in the USA
LVHW091923220122
708967LV00004B/517